THE DRAFT TREATY FOR THE ESTABLISHMENT OF THE EAC: A CRITICAL REVIEW

Edited by

Sengondo E.A. Mvungi

DAR ES SALAAM UNIVERSITY PRESS LTD.

Published by:
Dar es Salaam University Press Ltd.,
P. O. Box 35182,
Dar es Salaam.
TANZANIA.

ISBN 9976-60-366-5

This book has been published with the financial support of the University of Dar es Salaam Directorate of Research and Publications and the Programme Management Unit (PMU-2000) which financed the University Study Team on the Draft Treaty for the Establishment of the East African Community. It is the report of the Study Team, upon which this book is based.

CONTENTS

PREFACE

This book is a result of an interdisciplinary study conducted by scholars of the University of Dar es Salaam on the draft treaty for the establishment of the East African Community. The scholars who have contributed to this volume were member of a study team appointed by the Vice Chancellor of the University of Dar es Salaam, Professor Matthew Luhanga, to assist the government of the United Republic of Tanzania in providing input to the final treaty for the establishment of the East African Community.

The treaty was signed on 30th November 1999 and finally came into force on the 7th July 2000. Through this treaty the long-awaited East African Community has come into existence. Most of its organs including the Legislative Assembly and the East African Court have already taken shape. The new Community has once again raised the hopes of the people of East Africa that the region will once again become one. It is noteworthy to mention the copious similarities of the new treaty with the old one. Some salient features of the old treaty have been retained not because of their necessity or importance but because they touch upon the sensitive question of how much power the leaders of the Partner States are ready to surrender to the community.

The fact is that not much ground has been covered in terms of surrender of sovereign power to the new body. At least for the time being the Summit retains a veto power over legislative acts of the community. If the community is to be meaningful to the people of East Africa, Article 63(4), which empowers a Head of state to withhold assent, must be removed. A people-centred Community can hardly be achieved if we must still retain such obsolete provisions.

Another issue that needs speedy attention is the jurisdiction of the East African Court of Justice. The present treaty provisions are too narrow to satisfy the needs of an East African judicial system. Already the need for an East African Human Rights Convention and an East African Human Rights Court is a matter that needs urgent attention.

In any event, we are bound to celebrate the re-establishment of the East African Community, despite its weaknesses. In doing so I am expressing the sentiments of the contributors to this volume. There are hundreds of individuals who have worked selflessly for this goal and its realization is a great victory

The kind of integration and regionalism that we see taking shape in Europe, America, Asia and now in Africa indicate very clearly that borders are becoming less meaningful as economic constructs, when production is international and when affiliate sales are higher than exports and a large proportion of the existing flows are intra firms rather than extra. The question then to ask is with regionalism and integration taking place are we marching towards more protectionism or towards openness? The second aspect is to what extent can we really see regionalism and integration not only as means of efficiency and scale but also as means of bringing about sustained development? The last question is can regionalism and integration be sustained given the multifaceted historical, economic, social, political, cultural and geographical differences obtaining in the different countries that move towards such regionalism and integration. It is in the context of these questions and scenarios that we look at the current attempt to re-establish the East African Cooperation/Community.

THE HISTORICAL DEVELOPMENT OF THE EAST AFRICA COMMUNITY

Immediately Kenya and Uganda became established as political entities, close economic links were established between them and when British administration was extended to Tanganyika after 1918 it brought about close links with its two northern neighbours (O'cannor 1988). A common customs union was established between Kenya and Uganda in 1918, and Tanganyika became part of the union between 1922 and 1927. As economic development advanced, links were strengthened and formalized under the East Africa High Commission from 1948. So Cooperation became an important part of inheritance of the three East African states as they gained political independence in the years 1961-3 (O' Connor 1988).

With independence the three heads of state made declarations favouring political as well as economic union. However, between 1964 and 1967 the cry for political federation faded and even the economic Cooperation that had already begun to come to the fore suffered a lot of strains. The East African High Commission was replaced by the East Africa Commission Services Organisation in 1961 and under its auspices the common railways and postal system, financial and research managements, and customs union continued to operate with some modification. But various restrictions on trade between the countries were imposed and the common monetary systems was replaced by three separate currencies. In 1967 relations between the three countries improved and a Treaty of EAC was signed which provided for an Economic and Social Community. The prospect of the East Africa Community was expected to extend further to other countries (O'Connor 1988). The aim was to integrate countries such as Somalia, Ethiopia, Sudan, Congo, Rwanda, Burundi, Zambia, Malawi and Mauritius. In fact while Ethiopia, Somalia, and Zambia formally applied for membership of the new East African Community, Burundi, Malawi and Rwanda sent representatives to its in inaugural ceremony.

The synthesis of the above-captioned history indicates very clearly that the formation of the East Africa Community was not a one day process. In fact we can very quickly summarise the above history chronologically as follows:

- In 1922   -   The free trade area was transformed into a customs Union which had a common External Tariff.

  1923   -   Tanganyika joined the customs Union.

  1927   -   Free Transfer of imported goods was accepted among the three countries.

  1920 -1965   -   A common currency was issued and used in the three states.

  1930   -   Income tax systems were imposed for the first time in East Africa and they were harmonized throughout the three counties.

- The EAC was formed in 1967 and it superseded EACSO. The treaty called for official recognition of a common market and reorganization of common services.

- The community was formed when EACSO and the market were in danger of disintegration. The breakup of EACSO was seen by the member states as an expensive thing.

Efforts and chances of forming political federation at that time were not practicable and thus reforming EACSO was seen as imminent.

MOTIVES BEHIND THE FORMATION OF THE EAST AFRICAN COMMUNITY

With a little scrutiny, it becomes very clear that there were both general as well as individual (country) motives behind the formation of the East African Community apart from those social, political and economic infrastructures inherited at independence. Kenya had the aim of maintaining its outlet for exports of goods and services. Uganda on the other hand wanted to achieve a more balanced intra- East African trade and free access to the Kenyan market. It also wanted the institutional Headquarters in Uganda as a symbol of equality and given that it is a land-locked country it wanted to avoid being left alone in an unequal relationship with Kenya. As for Tanzania the aims were to end its overall net loss through cooperation in trade and common services, fo expand its trade and services on a regional basis and to search for a broader, closer and more planned market. Tanzania also aimed to find a practicable route towards regional and later on political Africanism.

At a general level, the aims of the community were to strengthen and regulate industrial and commercial relations which would accelerate development, the benefits of which would be shared equally (Malecela).

THE NATURE/CONTEXT OF THE THREE COUNTRIES AT THE TIME OF ESTABLISHING THE EAST AFRICAN COMMUNITY (1967)

Prior to this arrangement, the three states were British territories and thus they had a number of things in common:

* Similar political institutions.
* Similar school system.
* Similar judicial system, Government Administration.
* They had Common Services which were operated jointly.
* Had Common currency up to 1966.

Differences which existed include:

* Kenya had more inflow of private capital hence it was more industrialized.

* Kenya was also in an economically more strategic position; this was mainly due to its reletionship with the British during colonial times. The climate of Kenya was also good and attractive to foreign farmers.

* While Tanzania was socialist in orientation, Kenya was capitalist oriented and Uganda was neither of the two. The political and ideological differences which existed had a bearing on the survival/breakdown of the community later.

* Tanzania preferred control of investment and it even nationalized its major industries while Kenya encouraged foreign/western countries to participate in economic development.

- Kenya, unlike the rest, had more industries which were expanding very fast.

- The previous arrangements of cooperation, EAHC, EACSO, etc, all had their Headquarters in Kenya and were mainly dominated by Kenyan Administration.

The East African Community was formed in 1967 following a report by the Phillips Commission on EACSO which was investigating sources of unequal access to the benefits of the EACSO, Common Market, etc. (Mwase 1979).

The East African Community was also formed after an abortive attempt to form an EA Federation in 1963 (Mwase 1982). The main source of the failure was unequal benefit, which was enjoyed by Kenya particularly. Conflict over where the federal capital could be was another obstacle. As we indicated earlier the formation of the East African Community was seen as a stepping stone towards political unity of the three states.

AREAS OF COOPERATION

Areas of cooperation in the three countries existed before the establishment of EAC customs. The union existed from 1922 between the three and by 1923 there was free movement of imported goods.

Thus prior to independence East Africa had reached a level where it had common a Market though not formally established. The three countries had a common services in operation - Post and Telecommunication, Railways, Habours, Airways, Customs and Excise departments. Income tax, Directorate of Civil Aviation, Meteorological Department, Training Research Institutions and Higher Education also formed Part of EA Cooperation.

The establishment of EACSO in 1961 centralized administration of Customs and Excise, Revenue Currency, Land Seas and Air Transportation, Post and Telecommunication, Telegraphs, Education, and Radio (Mwase 1982). This was because for a long period before independence inter-country cooperation in East Africa was without significant institutionalization. The reason for this can be attributed to the presence of one colonial administration.

The community operated through free movement of factors of production (Capital and Labour) and a common External Tariff (Malecela 19).

AREAS OF SUCCESS

1. Collection of Customs and Excise and Income Taxes was centrally administered and hence the cost of collection was reduced.

2. Growth of Trade was recorded both with the East African Community members and the rest of the World.

3. The East African Community provided an internal market and protection for its own infant industries.

4. The East African Community negotiated with and become an associate member of the EEC which gave trading privileges to the East African Community member states.

The joint ownership and operation of East African Harbours and Railways, Airline, Post and Telecommunication Research Institutions, etc, provided employment to all member states.

The East African Post and Telecommunication was one of the few self sustaining financial organisations in East Africa. EAHC was the only corporation that supported its development budget from its own internal sources.

These successes of the EAC were translated into favourable social, economic and political developments of the region in general.

PROBLEMS FACED BY THE EAC (1967)

The problems of the East Africa Community can be traced back to the earlier arrangements (e.g. EAHC, EACSO) which it inherited. Mbogoro (1978) points out that EACSO had many shortcomings which resulted in a lopsided development among the member states.

Kenya dominated the East African common market which resulted in industrial and trade imbalances among the three members states. This was because:

• Nairobi was a more advanced industrial area, and well situated to serve the whole of East Africa.

• Kenya had a well developed infrastructure which tended to attract more investment.

• Kenya was bent on maintaining its advantageous position while Tanzania and Uganda were becoming more and more dissatisfied.

- Member states were also making decisions which tended to protect their national interests and not those of the East African Community. For instance, Tanzania introduced exchange controls, quota restrictions in inter-state trade, establishment of its national currency/Bank. Tanzania also forged a Union with Zanzibar, and politically she turned to the East European countries. (Mwase 1982). She also damaged Kenya's business interests with Zanzibar when she banned Kenyan heavy trucks from using her National roads and routes to Zambia. The Arusha Declaration which brought about nationalization of the "commanding heights of the economy" was also a heavy blow to the community.

- In 1969, Uganda launched a Common Man's charter which was a kind of move to the left. This strained its relations with Kenya. Uganda, Tanzania and Zambia belonged to the Mulungushi Club and Kenya was left isolated.

- The 1971 Uganda Coup which brought Amin to power was another powerful blow to the EAC. Tanzania refused to recognize Amin and wanted Obote back. Kenya accepted Amin; Tanzania did not. This provided room for the weakening of the EAC because the summit meetings could no longer be held and hence many decisions which concerned the community were left pending.

- The majority of people holding high posts in the community like ministers and directors also had their own national and political inclinations which in a way brought about the downfall of the community.

- The Heads of states formed the East African Authority but they had their own national interests as they were presidents of three independent nations. Before Bills were to become laws they had to receive consent from the three presidents and this was cumbersome (Nsibambi 1972:193).

- Conflicting monetary policies, exchange control and currency restriction also contributed to the downfall of the EAC:

  ♦ These conflicts were due to separate currencies administered by separate central national banks.

  ♦ Countries were required to maintain their currencies at par.

  ♦ The states were also required to harmonize their monetary policy for proper functioning of the community. All these brought conflicts.

FREVALENCE OF ADMINISTRATIVE/POLITICAL PROBLEMS IN RUNNING THE EAST AFRICAN COMMUNITY

There was also an underestimation that the community was an indispensable organization to the Partner States with enough immunity to withstand whatever shocks emanating from within or without. But some individuals from member states used different platforms to shake the community.

Thus the administration of the EAC also contributed to the breakdown of the Community:

- Time taken to reach decisions was unnecessarily long.
- Each member state had their own methodology, priority areas and strategies.
- Member states and the East African Community in general lacked a proper approach to coordination and integration of plans.

What is also clear is that Kenya became a net gainer in the East African Community. The East African Community had an arrangement for transfer of funds between the EAC corporations department and Headquarters. However, due to world foreign exchange shortages, transfers were not made (Mwase 1979), causing the situation between the three Partner States to become very tense.

A war of words was exchanged between states especially Tanzania and Kenya. Each country blamed the other on a number of issues, e.g., failure to transfer funds, unpreparedness to help others to develop, failure to ratify the 1964 Kampala Agreement on new industrial policy which aimed at allocating industries to countries in deficit. This led to unilateral action by Tanzania to establish industries in competition with those already in Kenya and to impose quotas against Kenyan manufactures (Mahiga 1976). Despite these measures Kenya still maintained its lead position in the EAC.

In summary then, it seems that the most serious problem that faced the East African Community was the unequal distribution of the resulting benefits among the three partners (O'Connor 1988). In fact it has been alleged that Tanzania lost more than it gained from the existence of the common market and Kenya gained the most.

ATTEMPTS TO SOLVE THE PROBLEMS OF THE EAC

As we mentioned earlier on, most of the problems which the EAC faced did not start with its establishment. In actual fact the creation of EAC was an attempt to solve the problems of EACSO including the transfer tax system, industrial and trade imbalances, concentration of corporation activities at the Headquarters in Nairobi and unequal benefits of the Common market.

- An attempt to correct imbalances in the growth of industries in the region started way back in 1964 with the introduction of a licensing system but it never worked.

- The distributable pool of Revenue was meant to help Tanzania and Uganda through financial transfers given the smallness of their work share in EACSO. This also did not really work.

- In 1975 EAC appointed an independent Commission to review the 1967 treaty. The commission was under one William Deams from the Caribbean and it presided over more of a disintegration of the EA community rather than a solution. One of its early observations was that countries were bringing proposals but which were being rejected by other members (Mwase 1979).

It is against this background that we would like to discuss the possibility, viability and prospects of re-establishing the East African Community.

PROSPECTS FOR THE RE-ESTABLISHMENT OF THE EAST AFRICAN COMMUNITY

Already many steps and advances have been made seeking the re-establishment of the East African Community. Different documents in the form of circulars, treaties, commentaries, including the East African Cooperation Development Strategy (1997-2000) and the Draft Treaty for the Establishment of the East African Community, have come into being. The Secretariat for the East African Cooperation was formed. Discussions are at present taking place in each of the three countries jointly to re-establish the EAC. Issues of common passports and a common flag in the East African countries have also been discussed.

From our own reading of the draft treaty and the discussions held in Kenya, Uganda and Tanzania we have a feeling that there are still challenges to the new East African Community and a number of questions which, if left unresolved, then the community, if started, will never be sustained. The first issue which arises is the basis of the community. Does this arise popularly from the mass population, that is workers and peasants, academics, civil society, business community, etc? It appears that there is little awareness of the draft treaty among the general population in Kenya, Uganda and Tanzania. In Kenya, for example, awareness has been restricted to the Ministry of Regional Cooperation, government officials and the business community. The same goes for Tanzania and Uganda. Few members of the academic community have even had access to the booklet of the draft treaty. The business community in Tanzania have just started discussing it.

The idea of the East African Community is a welcome one in the three countries going by the views of the people interviewed. However a lot needs to be done before the community is re-established. The pace at which the East African Community is now being established appears to leave many observes worried that the same mistakes that led to the collapse of the community in 1977 may be repeated. What lessons must we learn from history in order to produce a better East African Community? This is a central question which must be addressed. In fact an issue has been raised as to the viability of re-establishing the East African Community in the light of the COMESA and other global changes. Of course the other contention is that some member states belong to COMESA, SADC, etc., which will mean divided attention and allegiances. It is also argumed that while intra-trade in groupings like SADC are not growing that fast, trade with the rest of the world is more viable!! There is therefore the need to determine the role that the EAC will play in socio-economic development and its relationship with other organizations. What is unique in the new EAC that makes it important for Tanzania to join it and not merely stick to COMESA and SADC? What will be the comparative advantages?

Among the major barriers which are hindering and which appear to continue to hinder Cooperation at both formal and informal levels include inequalities in the structure of production, trade, income distribution and uneven development which still exist among the three countries. The experience of SADC shows that institutional mobilization of resources for regional development projects is very essential (Swatuk 1994) but then the members states have to enjoy equal gains.

The feeling among those interviewed indicated that the question of zero tariffs appears to be a major stumbling block with no agreement on whether it really should be applied and when the zero tariffs should begin. The recent Arusha meeting of top EA officials failed to break the deadlock. The meeting decided that a few industries (10%) will remain protected, but no list of industries was agreed upon. Nairobi (Kenya) with more industries appears to be pushing for zero tariffs. The indication is that Kenya will gain more from this exercise with countries such as Tanzania losing out. It is estimated that between 90-91 billion shillings would be lost to Tanzania per year. This makes it impossible to start zero tariffs in July. Probably the best way would be to work for ways in which zero tariffs would be applied for goods going to Kenya from Tanzania and Uganda and those from Kenya to Uganda and Tanzania be taxed, at least for an agreed period of say five to ten years, until we have at least a near to equitable growth among the three members.

The central issue for future East African Cooperation is how to harmonize industrial strategies in the East African Countries and to determine what will be achieved together and by each individual country. When it comes to the tourist industry, for instance, there seems to be a big disagreement on how to cooperate in that, because of the existing and envisaged imbalance among the three countries, Kenya will be the only winner. It seems that the Kenyan tourist industry is more developed than that of Tanzania and although Tanzania has a lot of potential she seems to be the loser. What has not been streamlined is how will Tanzania and Uganda benefit equally from and by the tourist industry.

From the Arusha meeting it appears that the treaty is to be to signed in July 1999 as a principled document and to have protocols after signing. The uncertainty of implementation of the treaty became apparent during the Arusha meeting of EA leaders and officials.

The Aftermath of the Arusha meeting indicates that Steps towards Zero tariffs will not be achieved, leaving Kenya feeling very bitter after Tanzania and Uganda had refused to accept Zero tariffs.

Inequality/imbalance, particularly in the areas of trade/industrial development between the three countries, appears to be the main stumbling block hindering East African cooperation.

Efforts must therefore be directed towards removing or reducing these imbalances which exist between the three countries although our discussions with various people indicated that many in Kenya, particularly the business community, are not aware of these imbalances. The general argument being advanced by our Kenya counterparts is that in one way or another, each country will benefit from the introduction of zero tariffs. In this regard the move towards zero tariffs must be explored in greater detail. It is suggested that the three countries identify strengths and weaknesses in economic and social development in each country and then work towards removing the imbalances.

It is also suggested that political developments in the three countries will also affect EA cooperation. Political instability or uncertainty is likely to have an impact on the sustainability of EA cooperation. It is therefore in the interests of the three countries to sort out their political differences and to base EA cooperation outside the realm of political leaders. Lessons from the history of EA cooperation must be revisited for the success of future EA cooperation. For instance, transformation of Kenyan policies is unpredictable after the 2002 political elections which will see the departure of President Moi from the political limelight. Armed conflict and increasing political instability in Uganda is also likely to affect future EA cooperation. The relationship that exists between Uganda and Burundi and Rwanda is rather worrying particularly if the latter two would like to join the community later on. Tanzania thus needs to have a more critical approach to EA cooperation due to political strifes, conflicts and instability/uncertainty of the neighboring countries and indeed within its own boundaries. The introduction of multi-party politics in Kenya and Tanzania and absence of parties in Uganda point to difficulties of joint agreement at the political level.

Industrial and agricultural production in Tanzania is still very low and this compounds the imbalance with Kenya and Uganda which is likely to affect EA cooperation. It is suggested that the potential of each country be developed into a major asset. For instance, Tanzania should strive to develop its agricultural capability due to availability of large areas of productive land and water bodies (lakes, rivers, etc.) Tanzania could then become the granary of East Africa. Focus should also be on marketing and transportation of agricultural goods as well as movement of people and capital. The movement (free) should be such that it benefits all. These issues are not simple and hence need serious sorting out.

The future success of East African cooperation will also rest on the extent to which the three East African countries will share their natural resources, particularly those from water bodies, for the development of East Africa. If the three countries can pool their resources in all key sectors, each helping the other and each willing to sacrifice something for the good of the other and for the benefit of all, then the prospects of EA cooperation will be enhanced. Loopholes in sharing have to be ironed out for effective EA cooperation. Strategies for developing common resources must also be developed. The mining industry is a case in point. Tanzania and Uganda have the potential to develop a strong mining sector, but they cannot do this alone.

If there is to be common movement of people and resources in East Africa then issues such as land policies have to be addressed. At present each country has different land regulation/laws and as such it is impossible for people to settle in different parts of East Africa and to carry out trade and other business. A common judiciary system for East Africa is also required. Otherwise interactions between EA will not bear fruit and movements of people will remain limited.

Before the treaty is signed and put into effect Tanzania needs to examine critically the extent to which the EA cooperation will contribute to addressing key development issues/problems. These include growing mass poverty, deteriorating social conditions and high unemployment rates. The central issue must be how best can the three East African states put to use their comparative advantages for the development of the East African community. There is a need to highlight and identify how EA cooperation will contribute to the development process of the individual East African countries and as a region. The issue of equal partnership between the three countries must be the underlying thrust of all efforts towards the creation of a viable East African community.

The general public must feel that they are part and parcel of efforts to create a stronger East African community if it is to function effectively. It is fair to conclude that at the moment the EA Draft Treaty has not clearly identified what role the people of East Africa will play in EA cooperation. The drafting of the treaty and present efforts to put it into effect have involved only the political leaders of the three governments. It cannot be over-emphasized that all key decisions regarding EA cooperation must include the general public. This has yet to be achieved and stands as a major stumbling block towards EA cooperation. A referendum would have been a proper channel for the establishment of the East African Community. We feel that there is still time and people should be given the opportunity to debate it.

On education, the three East African states need to overcome serious discrepancies in the educational system, particularly in Kenya where they follow the 8-4-4 system which is different from that of Tanzania and Uganda. This hinders movement of students within EA. Efforts must be made that develop common syllabuses and institutional set-up which will need a lot of details to be worked out.

The educational sector offers perhaps the best avenue for East African cooperation. In the past a successful East African University had existed with three campuses in each of the three countries. The Inter-University Council has been in operation even in the absence of the formal EAC.

Renewed efforts to build on this must be identified by the draft treaty. The intellectual community is a leading force that must be harnessed for the development of the EAC.

Article 117 of the draft treaty on Development of human resources, science and technology outlines measures to foster cooperation in human resources development and in the development and application of science and technology within the community. Among other things it also seeks to enhance the activities of the Inter-University Council for East Africa and to encourage the mobility of students and teachers within the community. This is a positive step but the draft treaty needs also to look at ways to strengthen primary school education. Harmonizing the curricula and interaction of students and teachers at primary level can achieve this objective.

In the field of health it is suggested that health resources of the three East African countries be mobilized and pooled together. This includes medical personnel, referral hospitals and other health centres.

The development of specialized health facilities to be used jointly instead of each country establishing its own facilities would also further EA cooperation.

What we are positing here is that there are a number of things which must be carefully sorted out before the community can be launched.

CONCLUDING REMARKS

As we indicated right from the outset the world is moving from national markets to international/global markets. We also indicated that while globalization is picking up with moves toward regionalism there are also moves towards fragmentation as a result of conflicts and global crises. It is true that there are those who see regional grouping as a building block which will facilitate multilateralism while others see this move as a stumbling block which will lower international trade (it only regionalises it) hence reducing competition (Kobbin 1995). In re-establishing the EAC we need to address the above-mentioned scenarios so that both protectionism and openness within the global economy are rationalized and harmonized in the interests of the three countries as a whole as well as the individual countries.

Our thinking is that, as countries are implementing the structural adjustment policies, with globalization demanding full liberalization of trade (anti-protectionism) and with the removal of customs duties and removal or reducing subsidies for agriculture, the implementation of the establishment of the East African Community is definitely bound to be affected either negatively or positively – on an individual country basis. The free international market poses a big challenge to the East African Community (Courie 1997).

One of largest challenges of the East African Community which needs to be addressed much more squarely before the signing of the treaty is the role of the state and the private sector. The former is being reduced while the latter is taking the upper hand under the adjustment processes. The renewed cooperation has to incorporate this element in a much more strategic manner, as it is likely to be the leading sector. This is a very intricate issue and plans to involve them right from the beginning cannot be over-emphasised. The private sector should grow with the new East African Community (Corrier 1997) without necessarily relegating the role of the state to the background. The state must remain as an effective overseer with the necessary powers and infrastructure to make reforms particularly because we already have unequal development of the private sector in the three countries given the nature and context of their historical, political and economic development. The pace of the development of the private sector has been different in the three countries, that of Kenya moving faster than that of the other two countries, thereby gaining more experience.

In the final analysis we think the renewed East African Community is essential but the national, regional and global environment in which the establishment is taking place should be properly analysed. We also feel that this should be gradual given that the three countries do not have common policies that are fully established. There is a need to start on a case-by-case basis removing one barrier after another and harmonizing different facets. Integration should not be forced on people – the aspects of integration which are social, economic and political should be seen evolving making it easier to subjectively and objectively capitalize on them (Corrier 1975). Let us give all the stakeholders more time as we believe that the process of the re-establishment of the community is moving too fast.

BIBLIOGRAPHY

Alan R. Roe" The Impact of the East African Treaty on the Distribution of S.E.A.C.S.O BENEFITS. ERB Paper 67-15 November 1967.

A.M. O'Connor "A Wider East African Economic Union? Some Geographical Aspects" The Journal of Modern African Studies, 6,4 (1968), pp. 485-493.

A.P. Mahiga "National Development Strategies and Regional Integration: Tanzania and Kenya in the East African Community" Taamuli, A Political Science Forum Vol. 6 December 1976.

Apolo Robin Nsibambi "Political Commitment and Economic Integration: East Africa's Experience" The African Review Journal Volume 2 Number 1, 1972.

Article in, "The European Community in brief "The Courier No. 48-March AP 1975.

Brjon Hettne and Fredrik Soderbaum "The New Regionalism Approach" Politeia Volume 17 No. 3, 1998 pp. 6-21.

Brjon Nettne "Globalism, Regionalism and the Europeanization of Europe" Politiea volume 3 1998 pp. 48-59.

David Foff and George Von Der Muhll "Political Socialization in Kenya and Tanzania - A Comparative Analysis" The Journal of Modern African Studies, 5-1 (1967) pp. 13-51.

Dennis L. Dresang and Ira Sharkansky "Public Corporations in Single-Country and Regional settings: Kenya and The East African Community" International Organization Journal Volume 34 No. 2, 1980.

East African Cooperation Development Strategy (1997-2000) Permanent Tripartite Commission for the Establishment of the East African Community.

Fredrik Soderbaum "The New Regionalism in Southern Africa". Politeia Volume 17 No. 3, 1998 pp. 75-94.

Larry A. Swatuk "Prospects for Regional Integration in Post-Apartheid Southern Africa. Journal of the 3rd World Spectrum Volume 1. No. 2 falls 1994. Page 17-35.

Ngila Mwase "East African Federation: The End of an Illusion? Paper Taamuli, Political Science Forum Volume II Number 2, 1982.

Ngila Mwase "Regional Economic Integration and the Unequal Sharing of Benefits: Background to the Disintegration and Collapse of the East African Community" Africa Development Volume 4 number 2 and 3, 1979.

Peter Robson, George Allen & Unwin, "Evolution and Relevance of Inter country Cooperation in East Africa. Foreign Assistance and East African Common Services during the 1960s Weltforum Verlag MUCHEN 1975.

Reginald Herbold Green "The East African Community: A Valediction forbidding Mourning" The African Review a Journal of Africa Politics, Development and International Affairs Volume 8 Number 1 and 2, 1978 pp. 1-187.

Robert Kennedy, "East African cooperation on safer ground?" Africa Confidential Journal No. 13 July 1, 1966.

Stephen J. Bobrin "Regional Integration in Globally Networked Economy" Transitional Corporations, Journal Volume 4, number 2. (August 1995) pp. 15-32.

Summary Brief on COMESA, Com/Brief/98/2/.

Susan Aurelia Citelson "Can the UN be an Effective Catalyst for Regional Integration? The Case of the East African Community" The Journal of Developing Areas 8 (October 1973) pp. 65-82.

Treaty of the Southern African Development Community – September 1992.

2

POLITICAL ANALYSIS OF THE DRAFT TREATY FOR THE ESTABLISHMENT OF THE EAST AFRICAN COMMUNITY

A.S. Kiondo[*]

INTRODUCTION

The world economy is today characterized by two significant processes, namely regionalization and globalization. These processes are not unrelated. Indeed they are either complementary or contradictory. Noting their contradictory nature, Polanyi (1957) has identified a double movement in which market expansion (globalization) is followed by society's reaction to protect itself from the impact. When this occurs, globalization is said to be challenged by popular demands for the return of accountability in politics regarding resource allocation and social welfare.

Following from the works of Polanyi (op. cit.) and Wallerstein (1974), Hettne (1997) has identified three different kinds of regionalism depending on the region's hierarchical position in the world system. These are neo-liberal regionalism, peripheral regionalism and western supported regionalism in the periphery.

Neo-liberal regionalism is found in the politically stable and economically dynamic core countries. It is pursued with the aim of improving the integration of the region's position in the world economy. It is therefore conceived as a stepping stone towards globalization. This type of regionalization is not contradictory but rather complementary to globalization.

* Associate Professor of Political Science and Public Administration

Peripheral regionalism occurs in regions where countries are politically turbulent and economically stagnant. Here, the leaders of such countries with or without the support of their people, could push for strengthened regional cooperation in order to counteract the process of marginalization and to increase their own capacity for conflict and resource-management. In this case, regional cooperation can result into the following: increased purchasing power and market expansion, followed by enhanced credibility with regard to political stabilization. Such outcomes could further enhance the peripheral country's/region's leverage vis-a-vis the outside world. Hettne (op. cit.) argues that this type of regional cooperation normally increases the possibilities of pursuing a more inward looking strategy, focusing more on internal security and development than on external relations. It is by nature contradictory to globalization.

Western support of regionalism in the periphery has a different motivation. Rather than supporting efforts for the achievement of increased intra-regional trade in the periphery, the motive is primarily to create larger internal markets in order to establish sub-regional cross-border free trade zones with outward-looking strategies. The resultant regionalization process is not contradictory to globalization but rather complementary because it is based on outward looking and external relations-oriented strategies.

From the discussion above, we can place the efforts for reviving East African Cooperation within regionalization at the periphery. The question that comes immediately to mind is: What form will the East African Cooperation take? Will it be contradictory or complementary to globalization? That is, will it be inward or outward looking? If the idea is to regionalize inwardly in order to minimize the negative impact of globalization, are there sufficient conditions for this?

Abrahamsson (1997:272) has identified three types of regional integration, capable of facing the challenges of globalization adequately. These are: (1) regional integration based on *strong-willed political elites* (2) regional integration based on *strong civil societies* and (3) regional integration based on *economic linkages* in the sphere of production. In each of these, African regional integration faces some constraints. Regional integration based on political elites is characterized by in-fighting and strong distrust among the elites. Apart from "in the border areas", civil societies' regional integration in Africa tends to be weak because the civil societies themselves are generally weak. Finally, economic linkages in the sphere of production are practically non-existent, a situation which greatly reduces the scope for increased regional commercial cooperation. This part of the report will focus on political cooperation as proposed in the "Draft Treaty for the Establishment of the East African Community and elaborated in the East African Cooperation Development Strategy (1997-2000).

POLITICAL COOPERATION: SOME THEORETICAL AND CONCEPTUAL DISCUSSION

According to the Draft Treaty, the East African Community intends to achieve a political federation by starting with a common market and monetary union. At the moment, the East African Cooperation could be categorized as being an economic unit in the state of becoming which, in the long run, is aimed at establishing a political federation. Political cooperation is just one among the various fields of cooperation that the Community intends to achieve. It is pertinent at this point to define political cooperation. In so doing, we will also try and differentiate it from political integration, political federation and political union. We will also try to explore the issue of why it is important, and why it is difficult to attain.

The above-mentioned concepts can be placed on a continuum with political union at one end, political federation in the middle and political cooperation at the other end. Political integration is the process of moving from political cooperation towards the other two points on the continuum. An elaboration follows. A political union is the ultimate goal of cooperating parties and entails a shared political jurisdiction in which the parties to the union agree to surrender either all or part of their sovereignty to a central political unit. A political federation on the other hand is defined as a "Union of groups, united by one or more common objectives, but retaining their distinctive group character for other purposes" (Friedrich 1964). In a political federation, each member state is sovereign in its own sphere. It should be emphasized however that even in their loosest form, federations require a certain degree of direct surrender of political jurisdiction to the federal authority (Hazlewood, 1967). Political integration is better understood as a process toward either a political union or a federation. According to Haas (1958:16), political integration is "the process whereby political actors in several distinct national settings are persuaded to shift their loyalties, expectations and political activities toward a new centre, whose institutions possess or demand jurisdiction over the pre-existing national states." Lindberg (1963:5) puts it more specifically that political integration is "a process limited to the development of devices and processes for arriving at collective decisions by means other than autonomous action by national governments". He further elaborates that political integration which involves a significant amount of collective decision making can be achieved without aiming at attaining a political union. Political integration permits member states to retain their identity and yet join in the organization that transcends nationality. Thus, political integration presupposes the existence of delegated decision-making. Haas (1964:11) concludes that "as the process of integration proceeds, it is assumed --- that interests will be redefined in terms of regional rather than a purely national orientation". Political cooperation involves mutual policy arrangements among member states aimed at attaining common interests and objectives. Unlike political union or federation, political cooperation does not necessarily require surrendering one's jurisdiction to the central unit. Political cooperation is a much broader concept and consequent process. It involves many more things without the intensity and depth of interraction entailed by federation and union. Following this distinction, while political cooperation among states may set out to ensure peaceful co-existence, friendship and solidarity as well as mutual respect for national sovereignty, etc., political integration towards federation, for example, may involve issues like establishment of collective institutions, development and implementation of common defence/ foreign policy, etc. However, it should be noted that political cooperation among member states is a prerequisite before a federation or union is established. Using marriage as a metaphor, while political federation/union constitutes a marriage, political cooperation is just friendship between partners. A process of integration can be equated to the engagement between two partners.

Both the Development Strategy and the Draft Treaty identify economic integration as the immediate objective of the East African Cooperation. Political cooperation is regarded as being an important means of facilitating economic integration and also as an end in itself eventually leading to the attainment of a political federation. It is important to point out the fact that economic integration can lead to the emergence of features of political integration as an unintended consequence. Lindberg (1963:44) points out four elements that can unintentionally lead economic integration to create potential features of political integration namely: if it leads to the development of central institutions and policies; if the tasks assigned to these institutions are important enough to concern major groups in the society; if these tasks are quite specific; and if the tasks are inherently expansive.

It is noteworthy to point out that the Development Strategy stipulates that cooperation will lead to the development of central institutions that are expected to make collective decisions initially in the economic sphere. In a way, the Partner States have to give up power to make decisions autonomously and unilaterally over certain matters. In addition, it is to be expected that there will be a development of policies and programs that are going to affect different categories of groups in member states. This will involve a change of behaviour of these groups in order to adjust to new institutions, rules and policies. Given all this, one can argue that the institutional set-up as well as stipulated policy priorities in the economic sphere provide the East African Cooperation with a lot of potential for unintended political integration. Thus, it is important to note and appreciate the fact that, while the East African Cooperation perceives itself as a cooperation, it is essentially in the early stages of a process of political integration.

There are several forces which facilitate the process of integration. Birch (1966:19) identifies social and economic factors. He points out that expectations of economic advantage and existence of social and cultural bonds which generate a feeling of community tend to create conditions for federal integration. Deutsch (1957) concurs with Birch by emphasizing that expectation of economic gains, a distinctive way of life and unbroken links of social communication constitute the important conditions for integration. However, history has shown that it is the political aspect that forms the basis for integration. This brings us to the importance of political cooperation in sustaining any level of integration. Its importance lies primarily in the fact that in order for any cooperation/integration to be established, there has to be a sense of political will, that is a readiness to be joined in an organization. This is a critical sine qua non. Also, it should be noted that a willingness on the part of politicians to participate in a cooperation or any kind of integration depends on the particular gains from the organization. Perhaps, it is safe to assert that there is a symbiotic relationship between political will on the one hand and anticipated gains to be generated from the collective organization on the other.

However, while economic integration has fared better in the various earlier cooperation schemes, political cooperation/integration has proved to be the most difficult goal to achieve. For many countries, a desire toward a political federation or union has turned out to be nothing less than an unattainable dream. Complexity of attaining political federation or even union stems from the traditional importance of the nation-state. In this regard, each state is supposed to be autonomous and sovereign. Unfortunately, the process of political integration goes against the phenomenon of sovereignty. As stated above, any kind of political integration requires a direct surrender of certain powers to the central authority. While each state remains sovereign in a federal integration, there is a general tendency for state politicians not to be willing to be subjected to a centralizing authority. The situation is made even worse when political leaders are compelled to protect the so called national interests. As a result, mutual compatibility of values, as Deutsch (1957) calls it, becomes difficult to develop. Besides, apart from social and economic gains, political, diplomatic or strategic gains come first in the minds of state politicians. As Birch (1966:29) clearly explains, when they are under no threat, external or internal, from which the state politicians hope that the integration might protect them, there will be a natural reluctance for them to surrender their autonomy. In addition, the will to surrender will be minimal when political leaders do not feel confident they would have anything but a subordinate role in the proposed federal government. Given its difficulties, political cooperation/integration needs a great deal of negotiations particularly on common interests in order to maintain the leaders' commitments and obligations. Haas (1974) calls this process the "upgrading of common interests". It is important to point out that regional cooperation, to use Solzhenitsyn's analogy, is like riding a bicycle. The rider remains on top as long as he is cycling. When he stops, he loses momentum and, finally the bicycle topples over. Thus, any kind of political cooperation/integration is likely to succeed only when the political leadership appreciates the fact that there are strategic gains to be made and works tirelessly for their realization. This is what makes political cooperation/integration critically important but also extremely difficult to achieve.

POLITICAL COOPERATION: THE DRAFT TREATY AND ITS DEVELOPMENT STRATEGY, 1997-2000

Current Arrangements for Political Cooperation

Political Cooperation is identified by the East African Cooperation Development Strategy (1997-2000) as "a foundation for cooperation in the

Economic, Social, Cultural and Security fields and ultimately as an end in itself" (p.41). The document maintains that political will and vision must be sustained throughout the key organs of cooperation in order to succeed. Treatment of Political issues is identified as one key "pre-condition to a viable and sustainable economic cooperation".

Three fundamental principles for political cooperation have been identified. These are: friendship, solidarity and good neighbourliness; mutual respect for national sovereignty and integrity, non-interference in domestic issues of member states, peaceful co-existence and peaceful resolution of disputes and conflicts, regionally as well as internationally. Finally, maintenance of peace, stability and security (pp. 41-42).

Objectives of political cooperation are identified as: reactivation of political cooperation; promotion of peace and security and good neighbourliness; increased liaison and contacts among the region's key political leaders and institutions; and lastly and ultimately political federation. Measures to ease border crossing are being implemented. An East African flag has been agreed on and hoisted. The introduction of an East African Standard Travel Document (passport) is well under way. Attempts have been made to adopt common positions on several complex issues including the political turmoil in Burundi and Democratic Republic of Congo.

Lastly five levels of contact are singled out. These are: Heads of State summit; ministers responsible for Foreign Affairs; Ambassadors and High Commissioners; Provincial/Regional/District authorities, and national Parliaments (p.42).

Most of the above are also contained in the *Draft Treaty for the Establishment of the East African Community (EAC; 1998)*. The preamble attributes the collapse of the East African Community in 1977 to "Lack of strong political will" among other factors. The objectives of the community include widening and deepening political cooperation [Article 4(1)]. Four and possibly five out of the six fundamental principles of the community in Article 5 are political: mutual trust and political will; peaceful co-existence and good neighbourliness; peaceful settlement of disputes; and democratic governance. There is thus no doubt that political cooperation is regarded as a core feature of the community.

Yet one needs to pause and wonder if the above conceptualizations of principles and objectives of political cooperation as well as the beginning of their implementation are enough, not only to sustain political cooperation, but equally importantly, to move us to political federation. An examination of the principles, objectives and institutions of political cooperation as outlined above reveals several theoretical/conceptual and institutional issues that we now turn to.

Theoretical/Conceptual Issues

First and foremost, it needs to be acknowledged that political cooperation enjoys a prominence in the current and envisaged community that was totally lacking in the East African Community Treaty. *The Treaty for East African Cooperation* (1967) did not mention political cooperation at all. One can only assume that it was included among "other relations" (p.2). It is not listed among the aims of the community. Clearly this is a notable departure from the old Treaty since the current Draft Treaty mentions political cooperation as one of its objectives.

Secondly, it needs to be pointed out that in the current Treaty, the political nature in the principles, objectives and institutions found in the documents are confined or restricted to political cooperation *Only*. Though political federation is said to be the ultimate objective, it is not mentioned in the immediate principles or objectives. Issues related to political cooperation are all easy to grasp or comprehend and even to implement. Everybody understands good neighbourliness, friendship, etc. Issues that are harder to comprehend, intangible, and of a long-term nature, are not included in the package. Political federation itself as a concept is neither defined nor explained. This is partly because it is difficult to give content to the concept and to sell it to the Partner States and the citizens as a whole for reasons already explained. Yet the cause of federation needs to be interrogated, questioned, debated and argued.

Thirdly and paradoxically, it seems that the objectives of political cooperation seem to work against political federation. Consolidation of nation states; non-interference in each other's internal affairs, respect for each other's sovereignty, etc., all work towards consolidating the status quo rather than easing the introduction of a new order.

While political federation is identified as the ultimate goal, the process that will bring it about is not specified, nor is there a timetable with clear benchmarks to guide the action. While we know the starting point and the end point, it is assumed the process of getting us from one to the other is obvious, but that may not be the case. Interestingly, while the process to economic integration is fairly spelt out, it remains to be speculated as to how the EAC is going to be intergrated politically. Even if it is assumed that federation will be the end result of a working political cooperation, including a defence relationship, that need not be so. There is a clear qualitative difference between the two, and how one gets from one to the other needs to be indicated, at the very least.

Institutional Issues

Institutionally, the envisaged set-up is a qualitative improvement on the old East African Community arrangement in several key areas. In addition to identifying political cooperation as a sine quo non for successive cooperation, the Treaty establishes several institutions that will further the cause of political cooperation. These are the Summit; the Council, the Coordination Committee, Sectoral Committees, the East African Community Court; the East African Community Assembly, and the Secretariat. In the Development Strategy, levels at which political cooperation would be realized are identified as: Heads of States Summit; Ministers responsible for Foreign Affairs, Ambassadors and High Commissioners; Provisional/Regional/District Authorities; and National Parliaments.

In both cases, we need to raise doubts over several issues. First is the phenomenal powers given to the institution of the Summit. A very domineering feature of the Summit is the extreme concentration of power in the presidency. For example, in Chapter Four Article 10(8), any member of the Summit may record his objection to a proposal submitted for the decision of the Summit and, if any such objection is recorded, the Summit shall not proceed with the proposal unless the objection is withdrawn. This sounds like the East African Presidents have a Veto in the process of decision-making in the community. As Nyirabu (1999:6) puts it, this style of decision-making is not very helpful in speeding up the process of integration. A simple majority rule would be more useful unless the issue concerned involved extreme national survival.

The second issue concerns the importance given to the Summit vis-a-vis the Assembly. Given the importance of institutionalizing ownership of the community within the population of East Africa, and of instituting a sense of their ownership of the same, the Assembly is one critical link between the community and the population. Yet it is marginalized to levels of less importance than the Summit and relegated to procedural issues. Its make-up also leaves a lot to be desired on several fronts. First, members of the

Assembly are to be elected not directly by the East African electorate, but by the National Assembly of each Partner State. Although those elected are supposed to represent the various political parties and shades of opinion, they still will not be direct representatives of the people. As a result, they will not have a constituency in the wider population to whom they will feel obliged to report back to, and to reflect their views in the Assembly. Also, since their election is a caucus process, it will not involve wide-ranging campaigns that will educate and even excite people in the community. This is a lost opportunity for the cause of the community to be known, its problems and prospects to be debated, appreciated and, hopefully, understood.

Related to the above is the number of the members of the Assembly. A total of twenty seven members from the whose of East Africa is too small. Again this revolves around the principle of representation that has been preferred. While one must be conscious of costs involved in having a larger body, still one must not trade off effectiveness against low cost.

Finally the set-up of the Assembly does not make it into a body that can step in and help when the Summit, for example, is paralysed for whatever reason, as has been the case in the past. Lacking an independent power base, members will have to tow the line of their respective parliament or the majority in those parliaments. The indirect election of the members of the Assembly is also a lost opportunity for parties to form and/or enter into alliances on an East African basis. Direct elections and the consequent campaigns would have meant formulating presentations and discussions of issues on an East African platform.

A second notable improvement on the East African Community arrangement is the allusion to the private sector. The role of the private sector in the development of the single market and investment area is described as critical. The East African Business Council is to be accorded observer status in the meetings of the commission and its subsidiary organs. A regional apex body for women organizations is to be formed to champion women's issues which are seen as important. Finally, regional-based organizations will also be encouraged for youth and professional organizations in order to mobilize civil society in support of enhanced cooperation. Yet even if these bodies are formed at regional level, it is not clearly spelled out how they will be involved in policy making. There is also no mechanism to ease the formation of these organizations at a regional level.

POLITICAL COOPERATION: VIEWS FROM EAST AFRICANS

The Committee managed to solicit views from well informed people who have no direct official involvement in the making of the East African Community, from Tanzania, Kenya and Uganda. They included political scientists from the Universities of Dar es Salaam, Nairobi and Makerere. Others included Ambassadors and other officials in Tanzania High Commissions in Nairobi and Kampala as well as respected members of NGOs in Tanzania and Kenya.

Several issues emerged from these views. One concern worries over the compatibility of the political systems of the three East African countries. While Kenya and Tanzania have multiparty political systems, Uganda runs a political movement otherwise known as "no party system." Among the fundamental principles supposed to govern the achievement of the objectives of the community by the Partner States is:

"Good governance including adherence to the principles of democracy, the rule of law, social justice and the protection of human rights" [Article 5 Section (d)].

Concerns were expressed that some of the Partner States had political systems that would not only be incompatible with others, but also would also not qualify in keeping the above fundamental principle, especially with regard to extreme corruption (interfering with good governance and the rule of law) and human rights record.

Related to the issue of political incompatibility is the issue of government structure and size. While both Kenya and Uganda have large cabinets (more than 60 Ministers and Junior Ministers), Tanzania has an average cabinet which stands at half the size of its partners. The three parliaments would also be composed differently. The Ugandan parliament would be composed of members technically belonging to the "Movement" but bearing attachments to the old political parties with their ideological beliefs. On the other hand, the Kenyan parliament has large numbers of opposition MPs who are nonetheless ethnically divided and poised. Tanzania has, on its part, a parliament highly dominated by MPs from the ruling party. The following table indicates the composition of parliaments in the three Community members:

Table 2.1: *Composition of Parliaments in Kenya, Tanzania and Uganda*

Country	Composition of Parliament		
	Ruling Party MPs	*Opposition MPs*	*Total*
1. Kenya	116	106	222
2. Tanzania	168	46	214
3. Uganda	All MPs belong to the ruling Movement		

Source: Compiled by the authors.

The nature of the parliaments would differ significantly and this might cause delays in some decisions that might be crucial to the community. For example, decisions from the Tanzanian parliament might be faster depending on the interests of the ruling party while in Kenya decisions might be delayed on the basis of a highly factionalized parliament. For it is said that, though the Kenyan parliament is shared more or less equally between the opposition and the ruling party, the opposition is highly factionalized along ethnic lines. On the other hand, the Ugandan parliament might be stronger due to the absence of visible party loyalties. This situation might result in quality decisions within the parliament, thereby resulting in favourable decisions for the community.

The second issue arising from the views of East Africans concerns the manner in which the Draft Treaty was conceived. There was an agreement among those consulted that the document came from above and not below. But maybe what was most important was that the signing of the document was delayed for a year (from 1998 to 1999) so that it could be discussed extensively all over the region. However, one year has now elapsed and the document has not yet reached the people of East Africa. Last year, the Secretary General of the Cooperation made available one copy of the Treaty to the East African Uongozi School at the University of Dar es Salaam. A Kenyan colleague secured a photocopy of the draft from us. A year later colleagues at the University of Nairobi still had the photocopy secured last year but have not yet seen the original document circulated.

The point made above is that, despite a one year delay in signing the document, East Africans have had insufficient opportunity to discuss the document which did not originate from them. Kenyans and Ugandans thought that they were worse off compared with Tanzania because there was a V.C. committee on the Treaty. But in Tanzania we did ask policy advocacy groups such as TAMWA (Tanzania Media Women Association) if they have discussed the document. The answer was, they have not even seen the draft treaty. It was only today that the Tanzania Private Sector Foundation (TPSF) announced a conference to discuss the Treaty on 22nd June 1999 at the Kilimanjaro Hotel (Mtanzania: 4 June 1999, p.12). TPSF has invited 42 of its members based in Dar es Salaam, 34 of its members from up-country and 12 Associate members mainly residing in Dar es Salaam. With the Draft Treaty expected to be signed in July, there is hardly any time left for TPSF to hold a conference on 22 June 1999 and hope to influence the document before it is signed. Given this type of lack of openness with which the document is handled, plus its top-down approach, it is imperative that some kind of referendum takes place before the document is signed.

The Draft Treaty talks a lot about "people-centred approach". One of its objectives includes "strengthening and consolidation of ... associations between the peoples of the Partner States so as to promote a people-centred mutual development ..." [Article 4 Section 3(d)] and one of its operational principles includes a "people-centred and market-driven cooperation" ([Article 6 section (a)]. However, in actual practice, the Draft is very weak in applying people-oriented approaches. We have already mentioned the weakness in vesting more powers in the Summit while marginalizing a people's institution, the Assembly; we have also noted the top-down nature of the Draft Treaty and its lack of openness and discussion.

Our last hope would have been vested in chapter 28 where the civil society is treated alongside the private sector. One would have thought that the document would, in this chapter, provide a mechanism for involving the civil society in the community's decision-making organs and activities. Instead, the chapter is much more focused on the private sector than the civil society. In fact the Treaty has no clear understanding of the concept of civil society. Rather, it seems to be market-oriented, pro-government and personality-driven. That is why it has to be signed in July whatever the case, in order to satisfy personal leadership styles and ambitions. The big questions to which answers cannot be found in the document are: How can the community be independent of governments? How can it be pro-people and people-oriented? How can it be depersonalized from the presidency and be predicated on the people of East Africa?

Finally, two areas are identified where the Partner States are required to immediately harmonize their policies. Specifically, the Partner States are called upon to "establish common foreign and security policies" (Article 131 Section 1). The area of foreign policy is very controversial within the three East African countries. To start with, Uganda is at war in the Democratic Republic of Congo. Uganda is also known to be leaning much more towards Rwanda and Burundi than towards Kenya and Tanzania. On its part, Kenya seems to have a vocal foreign policy towards international politics. Perhaps this is caused by open concerns expressed by International Human Rights Organizations and donor countries over Kenya's human rights record. On the part of Tanzania, maybe due to towing the donor line, the country has no controversial foreign policy positions. Within this context, one would think the area of foreign policy would be the last on which to expect common ground among the Partner States.

As for the security policy, again this is a very controversial area. Current discourse on security differentiates between the traditional narrow definition of security, based on political and military considerations, and the current definition which looks at security as a broad concept with human orientation. Within this broad concept, the security of states depends more and more on their capacity to satisfy the legitimate basic non-material and material needs of their populations (Abrahamsson, op. cit., p. 271). According to this definition, a more collective concept of security is justified by the fact that political and social instability in one country endangers the stability of neighbouring countries. Articles 132 (Regional Peace and Security) and 133 (Defence) of the Draft Treaty seem to be based on the narrow traditional definition of security mostly concerned with military and defence pacts and external threats rather than the broad human-oriented definition which makes more sense in the region where both Uganda and Kenya are faced with internal political and social instability.

To conclude this part of the report, it is noted that the overwhelming view of the East Africans consulted by this committee is that the Draft Treaty is, to say the list, very undemocratic in its inception (conceived from above than below), nature and approach towards the creation of the East African Community. The message one gets from this is that, rather than embarking on a false start, efforts should be made to facilitate open discussion of the Treaty among groups of stakeholders before the document is signed. Or if the Treaty has to be signed in July as previously arranged (again to underscore the rigidness and undemocratic nature of the process), then it should be signed as a document of intent, leaving out details of implementation to come in separate protocols.

CONCLUSIONS AND RECOMMENDATIONS

Several conclusions can be drawn from the foregoing discussion. First, political cooperation enjoys a prominence in the current thinking on cooperation in East Africa that was totally lacking in the old East African Community Treaty. Secondly, there is a certain degree of political will on the part of the leadership in East Africa to engineer meaningful political cooperation, even though the political will is based on individualized leadership wishes rather than an established public opinion. Thirdly and related to the above, the current leadership in the three Partner States deserve commendation for their support for political cooperation in the region.

The discussion has also shown that there are several areas where work still needs to be done to turn the hopes of political cooperation and even federation into a reality. First, the idea of federation needs to be closely examined, debated and interrogated. There is need to begin to develop different scenarios that it may take so as to familiarize the leadership and population with the possible choices, their costs and benefits. Secondly, there is need to develop a vision for political federation. This is critical in order to sustain and reinforce the political will. As already explained, political cooperation and federation is very difficult to achieve. The leadership therefore needs to engage in what we have called the "upgrading of common interest". It needs to be shown that cooperation is not only for the effective utilization of existing resources but also for the expectation of stimulus that it will engender in other areas. The idea of building a future economic bloc in Africa, promoting the region's bargaining power in international fora and building a strong regional political and military power base need to be explored.

Thirdly is the issue of process and strategy. Processes need to be explored inorder to bring about the envisaged closer cooperation, and ultimately, federation, even more so since, as already pointed out, the East African Cooperation in its present framework is already giving rise to the phenomenon of political integration. There is therefore a need to chart out strategies on how to cope with the consequences of political integration in an effort to attain a political federation.

Finally the various institutional arrangements of the community need a second look. The Assembly can yield greater benefits if it is people-centred. Also the various civil society institutions need to be assisted to associate on an East African basis.

After making the above general observations, the following specific recommendations can be made:

1. The Draft Treaty should not be signed hurriedly in order to please certain interests while jeopardizing its long-term potential. If it has to be signed next month, then it should be merely a document of intent with details to come later in the form of protocols.

2. Following from the above, a sustained open discussion should be invoked among important groups of stakeholders such as the parliament, trade unions, cooperatives, professional associations, NGOs, religious organizations and all other relevant civil society bodies.

3. Efforts should be made to make the end-product of the community inward looking, people-oriented/centred and socially broad-based.

4. Institutionally, the most important decision-making body of the community should be the East African Assembly elected directly by the people of East Africa rather than the Summit of presidents. This is not only because the Assembly is a much more democratic body, but also because the Summit made up of three members only can be quite unstable, unpredictable and capable of generating unnecessary friction.

5. The creation of the new Secretariat of the Community should be reviewed with the intention of making it more democratic. Furthermore, important positions in the secretariat should be vetted by the Assembly.

REFERENCES

Abrahamsson, H. (1997), Seizing the Opportunity: Power and Powerlessness in a Changing World Order, The Case of Mozambique, Padrigu, Gothenburg University.

Birch, A.R. (1966) "Approaches to the Study of Federalism" *Political Studies*, No. 1.

Deutsch, K. et al. (1957), *Political Community and the North Atlantic Area*.

Draft Treaty for the Establishment of the East African Community.

East African Cooperation Development Strategy (1997-2000).

Friedrich, C.J. (1964), "New Tendencies in Federal Theory and Practice"; Mimeo.

Green, H.R.H. (1978), "The East African Community: A Valediction Forbidding -Mourning" *The African Review* Vol. 8, No. 1 and 2.

Haas, E. (1958), *Uniting of Europe*.

Hazlewood, A. (ed), (1967), *African Integration and Disintegration: Case Studies in Economic and Political Union.*

Hazlewood, A. (1975), *Economic Integration: The East African Experience.*

Hettne, B. (1997), Development, Security and World Order: A Regionalist Approach, European Journal of Development Research, Vol. 9 No. 1, June 1997 p. 83-106.

Lindberg, L. (1963), *The Political Dynamics of European Economic Integration.*

Mukandala, R.S. (1999), "Political Cooperation," A paper presented at a Ministerial Seminar on East African Cooperation, at EAC Secretariat, Arusha, 25-26 March, 1999.

Mwase, N. (1978), "Regional Economic Integration and the Unequal Sharing of Benefits: Background to the Disintegration and Collapse of the EASC" *The African Review*, Vol. 8, No. 1 and 2.

Nyirabu, M. (1998), "Remarks on the Political Aspects of the Draft Treaty for the Establishment of the East African Community," A paper presented to the Tanzania Parliamentary Workshop on the Draft Treaty, Dodoma, 30th Oct. 1998.

Polanyi, K. (1957), The Great Transformation, Boston: Beacon Press.

The Treaty for East African Community (1967).

Tulya-Muhika, S. (1994), "Key Causes of Failure of the East African Community" in Abidi, A.H. (ed) *Revival of the East African Community.*

Wallterstein, I. (1974), The Modern World System, New York: Academic Press.

3

Economic Analysis of the Draft Treaty for the Establishment of the East African Community

N.C. Osoro* & W.E. Maro**

INTRODUCTION

There is an increasing pressure for signing the Treaty on the East African Cooperation by 31st July, 1999. At the same time there is a lot of discussion going on among different stakeholders about this issue. Both public and private institutions are involved in this discussion with one circle being totally pessimistic about the impact of this kind of cooperation on the national economy while another circle is totally optimistic about the positive impact. Yet another is in the middle but leaning more towards the optimistic side, if certain factors and/or conditions specified in the treaty are amended. The main objective of this report is to raise important issues for discussion with regard to the economic impact of the treaty. Specifically it addresses issues related to trade, industry (manufacturing), agriculture and tourism. Policy-makers need to discuss these issues at length in order to establish what exactly Tanzania wants to achieve from this cooperation.

We have to bear in mind that this is not the first attempt by the EA countries to establish some form of cooperation. In 1967, for example, the East African states signed the same kind of treaty which established the East African Community. This one was basically an economic cooperation arrangement. However, ten years later the community collapsed due to various reasons. These included, for example, difference in political philosophies which resulted in different economic policies. Other factors were the non-equitable

---

* Associate Professor of Economics, Department of Economics.
** Senior Research Fellow, ERB.

distribution of benefits emanating from the cooperation, poor compensation mechanism and crowding out of the civil society and the private sector from the community integration affairs. The latter affected Tanzania more because of the different political system. The main question to raise here is whether the treaty has adequately considered how to iron out these differences which may lead to the next collapse. One thing that can prevent this is the globalization process which started in the early 80's and which goes in tandem with the liberalization of the EA economies. This is a necessary starting point but not sufficient. There are still many diverse areas and a greater effort is needed towards harmonization for effective integration and equitable economic development.

BRIEF OVERVIEW OF ECONOMIC INDICATORS

Based on the 1998 figures, population in the three EA states nears 77 million people. About 38% of these are in Tanzania, Kenya coming very close with 36%. Uganda has only 26% of the total population. The total GDP of the three countries was estimated at 18.4 US $ billion in 1996 out of which 8.4 US $ billion came from Kenya (46%), followed by Uganda with 5.5 US $ billion (30%) and finally Tanzania contributing only 4.5 US $ billion (24%). The per capita income of Kenya is almost twice that of Tanzania. While the per capita income in Kenya in 1996 was US $ 310 that of Tanzania was US $ 160 and in Uganda it was US $ 280 (Table 3.1).

Table 3.1: *Basic Economic Indicators*

	Kenya	Tanzania	Uganda	Total
Population (1998)	27.5	29.5	20	77
% share	36	38	26	100
GDP (1996) ($bn)	8.4	4.5	5.5	18.4
% share	46	24	30	100
Income per head (1996) ($)	310	160	280	250
Manufacturing value added (1995) ($m)	976	107	259	1,342
% share	73	8	19	100
Cumulative foreign investment (1995) ($m)	443	73	23	539
% share	82	14	4	100
Exports (1996) ($m)	2500	696	623	3819
% share	66	18	16	100
Imports (1996) ($)	3500	1370	1231	5319
% share	57	23	20	100
External Debt (1996) ($m)	7.8	7.9	3.8	19.5
African competitiveness index (1998)	-0.17	-0.25	0.18	0.2

Source: World Bank, UNIDO, OECD, and IMF. BoT.

By 1995 the manufacturing value added from Kenya was almost 9 times that of Tanzania, and 4 times that of Uganda. During the same period the cumulative foreign investment in Kenya was 6 times that of Tanzania and almost 19 times that of Uganda. In 1996 the export share of Kenya was 66% compared with 18% of Tanzania and 16% of Uganda. The same phenomenon applies for imports.

This broad picture is indicative of the already obtaining unbalanced levels of economic development among the three East African countries. We will see more in detail when we discuss each individual sector, i.e. trade, industry, agriculture and tourism.

TRADE PERFORMANCE

General Trade System

Economic reform programmes have been vigorously pursued in the EA states over the past decade. In Tanzania the Structural Adjustment Programme (SAP) and the Economic Recovery Programmes (ERP I and II) have led to the gradual shift from the centrally-controlled economy to a market-oriented economy. It has, therefore, ushered in the participation of the private sector in production, trade, commerce and finance. The emerging private sector is, however, still weak and inexperienced to the extent that it cannot as yet compete with the well-established private sector in the other two Partner States, especially Kenya. Further market reforms, promotion of the private sector and capacity building are the important areas that need continued government attention and support.

The overview of indicators above show the position of one year as far as trade is concerned. However, more historical data show the same trade pattern. Looking at the general trade system of the three countries between 1975 and 1991 (17 year series) we see that imports by Kenya average 57%, while that of Tanzania and Uganda trail by 32% and 11% respectively. (Table 3.2). Fig .3.1 clearly shows the leading position of Kenya relative to the other states as far as imports are concerned. The figure shows also that this disparity was apparent even before the collapse of the EA community in 1977. In the early 80's imports into Kenya show an increasing trend while that for Tanzania is vice versa. Even the trend in Uganda, though still below that of Tanzania, is increasing during this period.

Table 3.2: *Total Trade of the EA Countries (1975-1991): IMPORTS*

Year	Tanzania	Kenya	Uganda	Total
1975	773	980	200	1953
1976	646	973	170	1789
1977	748	1284	190	2222
1978	1143	1710	255	3108
1979	1084	1657	197	2938
1980	1246	2603	293	4142
1981	1175	2085	39	3299
1982	1131	1603	350	3084
1983	805	1358	350	2513
1984	836	1526	331	2693
1985	1055	1457	342	2854
1986	876	1650	380	2906
1987	875	1738	583	3196
1988	805	1987	532	3324
1989	998	2163	578	3739
1990	698	2041	551	3290
1991	1170	2101	523	3794
AVERAGE	944.9	1700.9	344.9	2990.8
% Share	31.6	56.9	11.5	100.0

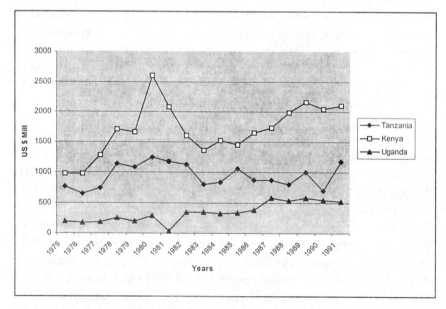

Fig. 3.1: *Total import value of the three EA countries, 1975-91, (US$ Mill.)*

This historical data depicts the same pattern for exports. Over the same period Kenya is far ahead by almost two thirds (66%). The average share for Uganda is about 20% while Tanzania trails behind with only about 14%. (Table 3.3) the disadvantaged position of Tanzania is self-explanatory.

Table 3.3: *General Trade System (1975-91) US $ mill: EXPORTS*

Year	Tanzania	Kenya	Uganda	Total
1975	89	644	268	1001
1976	95	825	359	1279
1977	63	1195	347	1605
1978	107	1922	387	2416
1979	112	1107	436	1655
1980	133	1419	345	1897
1981	153	1199	242	1594
1982	455	977	372	1804
1983	383	983	377	1743
1984	379	1083	409	1871
1985	341	989	405	1735
1986	323	1217	423	1963
1987	268	961	333	1562
1988	269	1072	300	1641
1989	373	1176	298	1847
1990	331	1120	190	1641
1991	360	1118	196	1674
AVERAGE	**249.1**	**1118.1**	**334.5**	**1701.6**
% Share	**14.6**	**65.7**	**19.7**	**100.0**

Again, graphically, we see that Tanzania is in bottom position even before 1977, the year of the collapse of the EA community. Indeed there was a declining trend of exports from Tanzania between 1982 and 1988 (Fig. 3.2). The imports were declining at an average annual rate of about 0.83%.

Trading Within the EA Region

The foregoing section discusses the general trade performance. It is now worth observing the performance within the EA Region where the trading imbalance can better be discerned. Tanzania's trade with Kenya and Uganda

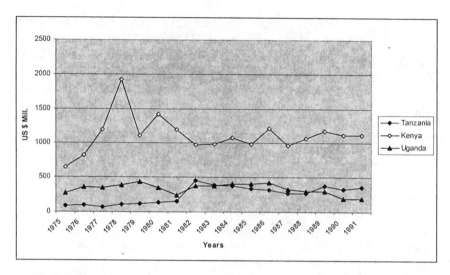

Fig 3.2: *Total Export values of the three EA countries, 1975-91 (US$ Mill)*

between 1978 and 1987 can be observed in Table 3.4. First, looking at the imports, we see that during this period imports from Kenya amount to an average of 88% while the same from Uganda were only about 12% on average.

Table 3.4: *Tanzania's Trade with her Neighbours (1978-87) ('000 US $) Jan-Dec*

Year	Imports					Exports				
	Kenya	Uganda	Total	% Kenya	% Uganda	Kenya	Uganda	Total	% Kenya	% Uganda
1978	3473	3	3476	99.91	0.09	112	191	303	36.96	63.04
1979	11045	98	11143	99.12	0.88	214	12404	12618	1.70	98.30
1980	9715	103	9818	98.95	1.05	111	14724	14835	0.75	99.25
1981	9523	103	9626	98.93	1.07	319	8235	8554	3.73	96.27
1982	12354	100	12454	99.20	0.80	1182	900	2082	56.77	43.23
1983	8663	5984	14647	59.15	40.85	700	2380	3080	22.73	77.27
1984	7651	12229	19880	38.49	61.51	4290	3170	7460	57.51	42.49
1985	20650	2750	23400	88.25	11.75	1000	1810	2810	35.59	64.41
1986	36610	1660	38270	95.66	4.34	3040	5550	8590	35.39	64.61
1987	26000	150	26150	99.43	0.57	7330	2620	9950	73.67	26.33
Average	14568	2318	16886	87.71	12.29	1830	5198	7028	32.48	67.52

Source: Economic Commission for Africa Foreign Trade Statistics for Africa, Direction of Trade A No. 32, 1990

On the export side, the decade's average shows that about 68% of Tanzanian goods were exported to Uganda compared with about 32% that were exported to Kenya. This indicates that our market concentration is more in Uganda than Kenya while we are a big market for Kenyan goods.

The trade imbalance was observed even in the late 70's and early 80's after the closure of the border between Tanzania and Kenya after the collapse of the EA community. The level of imbalance was more or less constant over the first 7 years. However, sharp differences increased after the liberalization of trade in the mid 80's (See Fig. 3.3). As will be seen later, these imbalances continued to grow in the 90's.

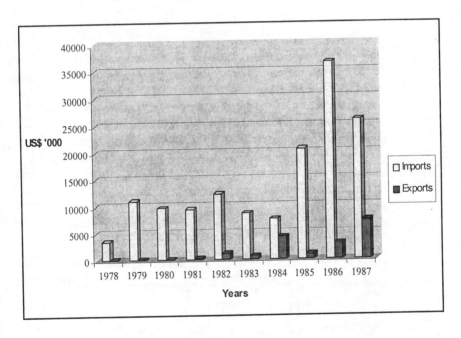

Fig 3.3: *Tanzania's Import and Export Values from and to Kenya (US$ '000)1978-87*

Regarding Tanzania is trade with Uganda, though still unequal, there are signs of harmonization especially in the late 80's. Fig. 3.4 shows that a stark imbalance existed in the late 70's. More was exported to Uganda, maybe as a result of the war with Uganda during this period. The situation changed in the early 80's when Tanzania was importing more from Uganda (Fig.3.4). At least trade is not typically unidirectional as is the case with Kenya.

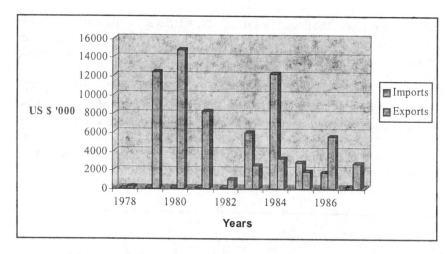

Fig 3.4: *Tanzania's Import and Export values to Uganda (1978-87) (US$ '000)*

To have a clearer picture of the trade imbalances, let us observe Kenya's trade pattern with her neighbouring countries over the same period, i.e. 1978-87, where comparable figures are available. Table 3.5 below shows that of Kenya's total imports, about 40% originate from Tanzania while 60% is from Uganda on average. On the export front, Tanzania exports only about 6% to Kenya relative to 94% from Uganda.

Table 3.5: *Kenya's Trade with Her Neighbours ('000 US $) Jan-Dec*

Year	Imports					Exports				
	Tanzania	Uganda	Total	% Tanzania	% Uganda	Tanzania	Uganda	Total	% Tanzania	% Uganda
1978	914	5111	6025	15.17	84.83	0	81370	81370	0.00	100.00
1979	274	2150	2424	11.30	88.70	0	81775	81775	0.00	100.00
1980	535	3257	3792	14.11	85.89	2106	149565	151671	1.39	98.61
1981	611	2253	2864	21.33	78.67	587	104447	105034	0.56	99.44
1982	1530	2474	4004	38.21	61.79	1237	94780	96017	1.29	98.71
1983	1526	1285	2811	54.29	45.71	1585	94323	95908	1.65	98.35
1984	4190	1595	5785	72.43	27.57	1126	94188	95314	1.18	98.82
1985	2085	3150	5235	39.83	60.17	1066	95409	96475	1.10	98.90
1986	2729	2659	5388	50.65	49.35	33604	89537	123141	27.29	72.71
1987	4175	1103	5278	79.10	20.90	23790	84785	108575	21.91	78.09
Average	**1857**	**2504**	**4361**	**39.64**	**60.36**	**6510**	**97018**	**103528**	**5.64**	**94.36**

Source: Economic Commission for Africa Foreign Trade Statistics for Africa, Direction of Trade A No. 32, 1990

Again figures 3.5 and 3.6 that follow help to demonstrate the clear trade imbalance unfavourable to Tanzania.

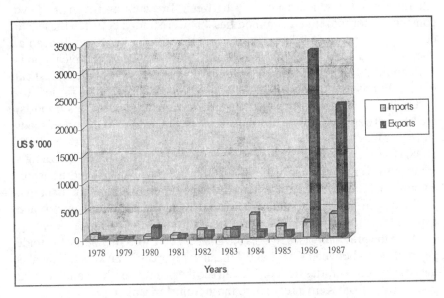

Fig 3.5: *Kenya's Import and Export Values from and to Tanzania, 1978-87 (US $ '000)*

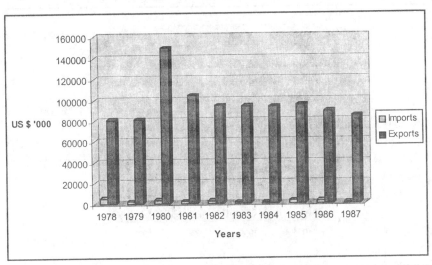

Fig. 3.6: *Kenya's Import and Export Values from and to Uganda, 1978-87 (US $ '000)*

One would tend to think that this trade imbalance was more pronounced in the early and late 80's. We argue that even in the early and mid 90's the situation has worsened especially between Tanzania and Kenya. If we consider major individual commodities that were traded between these two countries in the 1994-97 period, we find that of all exports to Tanzania, manufactured goods are leading by about 30% followed by chemical goods with about 20%. This means more than 50% of all exports are industrial goods. Foods and beverages together account for about 22% (Table 3.6).

On the other hand, Tanzania's exports to Kenya (i.e. Kenya's imports) are basically agricultural. In absolute terms the total value of export of foods and beverages is about 20% of those of Kenya, i.e Kshs Mill 520 against Kshs 2608. However, food and beverages account for about 60% of all Tanzania's exports to Kenya. Crude materials take up 22%, machinery and transport equipment 17% (even here the majority is re-exports), while manufactured goods account for only about 0.5%. In total, of all traded goods (imports and exports together) more than 90% are exports from Kenya to Tanzania.

As in the previous cases figures 3.6 and 3.7 serve to demonstrate the trade gap that exists between Kenya and Tanzania. Figure 3.7, however, indicates the type of commodities traded. We can see the position of the manufactured goods (MG) from Kenya relative to those from Tanzania.

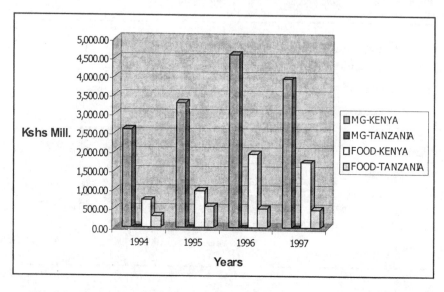

Fig. 3.7: *Trade of Selected Commodities Between Kenya and Tanzania (1994-97)*

Economy Analysis of the Draft Treaty

Table 3.6: *Kenya's Trade with Tanzania (1993-97) Kshs. Mill*

Description	1994 Value	1994 %	1995 Value	1995 %	1996 Value	1996 %	1997 Value	1997 %	Average (1994-97) Value	Average (1994-97) %
EXPORTS										
Food and live animals	742.23	7.38	991.52	9.06	1,953.28	14.39	1,733.47	13.47	1,355.12	11.08
Beverages and Tobacco	2,156.48	21.45	1,269.23	11.60	923.08	6.80	661.49	5.14	1,252.57	11.25
Crude materials, inedible	72.16	0.72	210.68	1.93	238.09	1.75	142.28	1.11	165.80	1.38
Mineral fuels and lubricants	488.03	4.85	423.15	3.87	927.51	6.83	1,028.84	7.99	716.88	5.89
Animal and vegetables oils and fats	597.06	5.94	1,112.77	10.17	1,077.40	7.94	1,431.22	11.12	1,054.61	8.79
Chemicals	1,883.93	18.74	2,400.29	21.94	2,577.19	18.99	2,568.73	19.96	2,357.53	19.91
Manufactured goods	2,605.19	25.91	3,302.93	30.19	4,603.78	33.92	3,939.36	30.61	3,612.81	30.16
Machinery and transport equipment	02.28	4.00	203.50	1.86	249.26	1.84	95.20	0.74	237.56	2.11
Miscellaneous manufactured articles	1,106.68	11.01	1,025.68	9.38	1,021.48	7.53	1,268.73	9.86	1,105.64	9.44
TOTAL	10,054.04	100.00	10,939.76	100.00	13,571.06	100.00	12,869.33	100.00	11,858.55	100.00
IMPORTS										
Food and live animals	304.32	25.66	570.83	72.46	512.57	58.12	495.10	66.03	470.71	55.57
Beverages and tobacco	146.15	12.32	3.56	0.45	2.17	0.25	45.53	6.07	49.36	4.77
Crude materials, inedible	310.87	26.21	153.74	19.52	249.85	28.33	112.08	14.95	206.64	22.25
Machinery and transport equipment	421.83	35.57	59.65	7.57	112.23	12.72	89.45	11.93	170.79	16.95
Miscellaneous manufactured articles	2.74	0.23	0.00	0.00	5.17	0.59	7.65	1.02	3.89	0.46
TOTAL	1,185.92	100.00	787.79	100.00	881.99	100.00	749.81	100.00	901.38	100.00
GRAND TOTAL	11,239.96		11,727.55		14,453.05		13,619.14		12,759.92	
Import as % of Total Trade	89.45		93.28		93.90		94.49		92.94	

INDUSTRIAL PRODUCTION PATTERN

The low level of trade with manufactured goods in Tanzania has been demonstrated in the earlier section which is explained by the low industrial base in Tanzania. Table 3.7 gives a few selected commodities that are produced in both countries.

Table 3.7: *Average Production of Selected Commodities in Tanzania and Kenya (1987-90)*

Commodity-	Average Production of Selected Commodities (1987-90)				
	Tanzania	Kenya	Total	% Tanzania	% Kenya
Beers (Mill. Ltrs)	52	317	369	14.1	85.9
Cigarettes (Million Sticks)	3002	6581	9583	31.3	68.7
Textiles (Mill sq. metres)	68	76	144	47.2	52.8
Cement ('000 tons)	587	1318	1905	30.8	69.2

Average production of beers, for example, indicates that between about 86% of this commodity was coming from Kenya and the remaining 14% from Tanzania. About 69% of all cigarettes were produced in Kenya. The same pattern is observed for textiles where about 53% originated from Kenya. We can also see that about 69% of cement produced came from Kenya. Both the trade pattern and industrial production show a great deal of imbalance especially between Tanzania and Kenya. It must be noted that these imbalances were not the cause of the earlier decisions to break the EA community. Hence this is an area that needs a careful approach in order to reach some form of adjustment before the treaty is put into effect.

AGRICULTURAL PERFORMANCE

Productivity

Even in the agricultural sector, the productivity of agricultural crops in Tanzania is much lower than in the other Partner States.

Of the three Partner States, Tanzania has the largest land area, population and water volume. It has larger forests and livestock grazing areas than Kenya and Uganda combined (Table 3.8). Comparable figures for cropland in Table 3.8 indicate Tanzania to have the least area cultivated. Figures for 1992-1994 indicate Tanzania as having only 4.4 percent of the land area under crops, Kenya 7.9 percent and Uganda 34 percent.

Table 3.8: *Distribution of Land and Population in the East African Partner States*

Partner State	Land Area ('000 ha)	Population		Land use ('000 Hectares)			
		No. in mill	Density per 1000 ha 1996	Cropland (1992-94)	Permanent Pasture	Forest Wood-land	Other Land
Tanzania	88359	31.3	349	3660	35000	33067	16632
Kenya	56914	28.0	488	4520	21300	16800	14234
Uganda	19965	20.3	1015	6780	1800	6300	5085
Total	165238	79.6	617.3	14960	58100	56167	36011
Tanzania as % of Total	53.5	39.3	56.5	24.5	60.2	58.9	46.2

Source: World Development Indicators 1998 CD-ROM, World Bank.

Tanzania has also about 35 million hectares which are suitable for grazing. It is reported that less than 40 percent is used by livestock keepers albeit not fully. With a livestock population of about 25 million (13 million cattle and 12.0 million sheep and goats), this gives an average livestock intensity of 1.4 per ha. In terms of domestic supply of livestock products, the opportunity for improvement is still great. About 50 percent of dairy products are currently imported. Per capita consumption of milk in Tanzania is 20 litres, in Kenya 44, Africa 35 and the average for the world is 105 litres. Likewise, the per capita meat consumption level in Tanzania is low, averaging about 10 kg.

In the area of water resources, Tanzania has the largest volume of water and the longest coastline compared with Kenya and Uganda. Estimates suggest that Tanzania is only second to the Democratic Republic of Congo (DRC) in water endowment. About 110 billion cubic metres of exploitable water per annum are available, of which over 75 percent is surface water. Not much of this volume of water is being used for irrigation purposes, despite having a potential area for irrigation of about 800,000 ha. The area currently under irrigation is estimated to be less than 20 percent (150,000 ha).

Another area where Tanzania could benefit from cooperation relates to crop yields. Major food crops grown in Tanzania are maize, sorghum, pulses, cassava, oilseeds, paddy, millet, sweet potatoes and wheat. Export crops grown include coffee, cotton, sugarcane, sisal, pyrethrum, tobacco, cashew nuts, tea, cocoa, etc. Apart from sugarcane, sisal and to some extent tea which are estate crops, the remaining crops are largely produced by smallholders. In either case the yields realized for both food and export crops range between 7 and 60 percent of the potential yield levels. (Table 3.9).

Table 3.9: *Current Average Yields and Potential Yields for Selected Food and Export*

Crop	National Average Yield t/ha	Potential Yield t/ha	National Average Yield as % of Potential
Food Crops			
Maize	0.6-1.5	4.0-8.0	15-38
Rice	1.5-2.0	8.0	19-25
Wheat	1.5	4.0	38
Sorghum/Millet	0.7	5.0	14
Sweet Potatoes	1.3-5.0	20.0	7-25
Export Crops			
Coffee	0.3	1.0	30
Cotton	0.2	0.5	40
Tea	0.9	6.0-9.0	13
Tobacco	0.6	1.0-1.5	60-40
Sisal	1.0	6.0	17
Sugarcane	70.0	150.0	47-53

Source: MALD (1993); Promoting Sustainable Agriculture and Rural Development; National Workshop on Implementation of Agenda 21, Dar es Salaam, p.40.

The picture provided in Table 3.9 above is explained by the use of low technology in production. With better technologies, agronomy and support services, there is ample opportunity for raising the current productivity levels by at least 50 percent.

Problems of the Agricultural Sector

There are many problems confronting the agricultural sector which are worth noting as Tanzania prepares herself to sign the Treaty establishing the East African Community. Only major problems are outlined below.

Absence of Technological Change

Both agriculture and animal husbandry are characterized by the use of low productivity human labour-dependent technologies with little use of agro-chemical inputs and improved seeds.

Low Awareness of Environmental Management

Poor conservation of resources, such as water and land, leads to their depletion or impoverishment. On the other hand, the inability to use agro-chemicals means that plants and livestock are left exposed to pests and diseases.

Poor Transport Services

Until recently (1996) Tanzania had about 75 percent of all rural roads (77,730 km) and 41.5 percent of trunk roads (10,282 km) in bad or very bad condition. This poor road network stifles marketing efficiency and hampers people's access to social and economic services like schools, markets, milling machines, etc.

Lack of Credit Facilities

About 50 percent of the rural people are poor and cannot therefore expect to finance their own capital accumulation. Without access to institutional credit, they cannot be expected to have enough savings to finance the capital needed to improve their output.

Inaccessibility of Women to Productive Resources and Support Services

Available information indicates that women in Tanzania produce about 70 percent of the food crops and are also heavily involved in export crops and livestock production. Estimates also point out that the ratio of males to females in the agricultural sector is 1:1.5. Despite the women's major contribution to agricultural production, their access to land, water, etc (*productive resources*), credit and labour-saving technologies is restricted, etc (*support services*). What is even worse is that they are deprived of income arising from production to which their contribution is the highest. Similarly, they have never been a focus of attention of the agricultural extension services. In this connection it is important to recognize that for a serious revolution in agriculture to take place, this major force, that is women, must have access to both resources and services.

Rural-urban Migration and HIV Infection

This is a major challenge to agricultural production and productivity because the able-bodied population in the rural areas is quickly being depleted. This challenge needs immediate attention by all Partner States in order to avert the increasing rural-urban demographic imbalance and the HIV tragedy for all East African Partner States.

Assessment of the Proposed Areas of Cooperation

There are many areas, which can form the basis of cooperation between Partner States in the agricultural sector. We have singled out only four because of their importance in enhancing agricultural performance.

Agricultural Research Services

This is an important cooperation area for the purpose of developing technologies and extension messages, which are relevant for the development of the agricultural and livestock sectors. Current productivity in Tanzanian agriculture measured by cereal yields per hectare are lower than in the Partner States (Table 3.10).

Table 3.10: *Cereal Yields and Average Annual Growth Rate of Agricultural Food Production*

Partner State	Cereal Yields (Kg./ha)		Average Annual Growth Rate of Food Production	
	1979-81	1994-96	1986-90	1991-95
Tanzania	1063	1310	0.9	-2.4
Kenya	1364	1822	0.9	3.2
Uganda	1555	1552	4.1	2.6
Average	1327	1561	2.0	1.1
Tanzania as % of Average	80.1	83.9	45.0	-218.2

Source: World Development Indicators 1998 CD-ROM, World Bank.

The productivity levels are subsequently reflected in the agriculture value added per worker and per hectare of agricultural land. The good research infrastructure available in the Partner States could enrich Tanzania's efforts in enhancing productivity in the agricultural sector.

Early Warning System and Agricultural Meteorology

The impacts of anomalous weather events go beyond national boundaries and have adverse effects on the societies of the region. Cooperation in this area of early warning system and agricultural meteorology would enhance food production and create food security in the Partner States.

Rural Transport

We mentioned earlier that roads and other means of transport and communications play a key role in market development and integration of rural and urban areas. Improvement of the rural transport network would play a significant role in agricultural production, in a country whose size is large and sparsely populated. Available data indicate that Tanzania's land area (88,359,000 ha) is about 4 times that of Uganda and 1.5 times that of Kenya. Opening up of rural areas would enhance the movement of goods, services and people to and from the rural areas. In the absence of this initiative, the majority of rural people would continue walking long distances carrying their crop harvests to the markets and whatever inputs they buy to take back home. The time spent on walking to the market and back home is wasted time in terms of production. The importance of cooperation in developing a rural network would go a long way towards making the agricultural sector more dynamic and productive.

Agricultural Financing

The major area of cooperation would be in extending loans for agricultural production, and in particular extending credit services to rural women to enable them to contribute more effectively to agricultural production. Related to this, cooperation could also take place in the provision of training in agricultural and cooperative banking as well as in establishing micro-finance institutions in the rural areas. In this regard, Tanzania can learn a great deal from Kenya's long experience in micro-finance and cooperative banking.

Management of Environmental Resources

The long-term sustainability of agricultural production depends heavily on how the available resources, that is land, water, forest, air, etc., are used. Since the three Partner States share common borders, wrong use of land, water and forests by one Partner State could easily affect the other. In order to promote better use of the available natural resources, cooperation in the use of natural resources would be an ideal way of reducing the dangers of environmental degradation.

Potential Benefits of Cooperation in Agriculture

Tanzania's agriculture is less developed than that of Kenya and Uganda. However, Tanzania is potentially rich in terms of natural resources, especially land and water. If an enabling environment were in place to exploit these potentially rich resources, Tanzania would stand to gain significantly in the cooperation. But, in order to enjoy the benefits of cooperation in the agricultural sector, two factors must be considered/resolved:

i) Solving the major problems stated above;

ii) Willingness to harmonize Tanzania's agricultural policies with those of the other two Partners States.

TANZANIA'S POTENTIAL IN TOURISM

Current Situation

In absolute and relative terms Tanzania has the largest number of tourist attractions compared with those existing in Kenya and Uganda. Almost a quarter of the country's total land area has been designated for wildlife conservation either as national parks, game reserves or sites reserved for environmental conservation. The country boasts numerous national parks including Serengeti, Ngorongoro Crater, Mikumi, Lake Manyara, Selous and Ruaha.

Tanzania not only has many national parks but these parks are also home to a variety of wildlife. The Serengeti national park itself has an estimated 4 million different wild animals and birds.

Other attractions existing in the country include marine tourism, in which a range of marine sports can be carriedout along the country's unspoiled beaches and in Zanzibar. Tanzania is also full of historical relics, archaeological treasures, as well as a variety of cultures, which attract tourists.

Earnings from tourism and the share of the sector in total GDP has remained low compared with Kenya (Table 3.11 and Fig. 3.1) and (Table 3.12).

Table 3.11: *Trends in Tourism Receipts in EA Countries (in US $ million)*

Country	1991	1992	1993	1994	1995	1996	% change (96-91)
Kenya	432	442	413	421	454	493	14.1
Tanzania	95	120	147	192	259	322	237.9
Uganda	15	38	50	61	79	82	446.7
Total	542	600	610	674	792	897	65.5

Source: Economic Surveys (various)

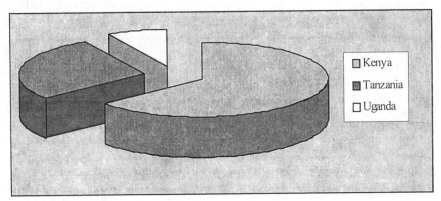

Fig. 3.1: *Average Receipts From Tourism in Kenya, Tanzania and Uganda (US $ mill) 1991-1996*

Table 3.12: *Tourism Contribution to GDP*

Year	Proportion of Tourism Earnings to GDP	% Change
1980	0.4	
1981	0.4	0.0
1982	0.3	-25.0
1983	0.3	0.0
1984	0.2	-33.3
1985	0.1	-50.0
1986	0.4	300.0

Year	Proportion of Tourism Earnings to GDP	% Change
1987	0.9	125.0
1988	0.9	0.0
1989	1.4	55.6
1990	1.5	7.1
1991	2.1	40.0
1992	3.3	57.1
1993	4.4	33.3
1994	4.7	6.8
1995	5.2	10.6
1996	5.5	5.8
1997	5.7	3.6
Average	2.1	31.6

Source: Economic Survey (1997, 1993) BOT, (1998)

Problems of the Tourism Sector in Tanzania

Despite showing growing trends, particularly in terms of increasing numbers of tourist arrivals and foreign exchange earnings in the 1990s, the tourism sector in Tanzania continues to face several constraints which contribute to the under-utilization of the sector's potential, as noted for example in Lyogello (1993), Okoso -amaa (1995), Semboja and Wangwe (1995), Mjema, Shitundu and Nyoni (1998) and Commonwealth Secretariat (1998). The main problems of the sector include:

i)   Dilapidated tourist infrastructure facilities, particularly the poor roads, aerodromes and rail network.

ii) Lack of core and specialized skills and management in tourism business

iii) Poor services rendered in some tourist hotels

iv) Poor marketing, i.e. inadequate publicity and promotion (campaigns) initiatives abroad.

v)   Slow process of divesting and privatizing the tourist parastatals.

vi) Low and unsustainable investment directed towards tourism, particularly in the areas of communication facilities, road network, the energy sector, external trade, private sector development and the agriculture sector.

vii) Lack of diversification and heavy dependence on the northern circuit. This means Tanzania does not utilize effectively the coastlines for beach holidays and the Southern circuit where the Ruaha National Park has a good population of elephants and the Selous Game Reserve has the largest number of wildlife. The Southern Circuit has, therefore, very high potential for hunting and could earn the country more foreign exchange because hunting (in Tanzania) yields the highest foreign exchange earnings per tourist compared with other tourist activities.

viii) Small domestic tourism mainly due to low income, low education, and inadequate special incentives for local demand.

ix) Lack of awareness and appreciation of tourist attractions by the community, including negative culture values.

x) Lack of institutional, technical capabilities and coordination among various ministries, the private sector and NGOs involved in tourism development.

xi) Inadequate sources of finance and financial institutions to cater for the development of the tourist sector.

xii) Poor coordination and land management for tourism development. The National Land Policy is yet to be implemented fully;

xiii) Lack of adequate tourism statistical information, and;

xiv) High tariffs and multiplicity of taxes on hotels, hotel accommodation, food and beverages, and tourism-related activities.

Assessment of the Proposed Areas of Cooperation in Tourism

The proposed areas of Cooperation are specified under Article 124 of the Draft East African Cooperation Treaty in which partners will undertake to:

"Develop a collective and coordinated approach to the promotion of quality tourism and wildlife management in the community and shall coordinate their policies in the tourism industry and undertake to establish a framework of Cooperation in the sector that will ensure equitable distribution of benefits".

Will Tanzania Benefit From Cooperation in Tourism?

Given the background of the potential problems and proposed areas of cooperation the next concern is, will Tanzania benefit from the Cooperation.

There are benefits and risks to be analysed first before answering such a question.

The Advantages of Cooperation in Tourism

The advantages of cooperation in tourism are those accruing from economies of scale. There will be, for example, a single tourism industry in the sub-region called East Africa and therefore a destination called East Africa. Tourists will have an opportunity to view a variety of tourist attractions in a destination called East Africa.

There will also be advantages in marketing the attractions abroad. The expanded tourism industry has the potential to create employment for Tanzanians as tour operators and other jobs in tourism-related activities.

The Risks of Cooperation in Tourism

i)   The major risk lies in the mechanism for ensuring an equitable sharing of revenue from tourism. The draft Article is silent on how the respective partners will *equitably* share the revenue from tourism.

ii)   For a number of years now the three countries have been pursuing different policies on tourism and the environment. Kenya, for example, with its relatively developed tourism sector has tended to pursue high volume, cheap mass tourism. In that course it has tended to over-use its attractions. In the Masai Mara Park, which is only 10% of the size of Serengeti, it has about 10 times the lodges of the Serengeti National Park. Tanzania and Uganda on the other hand have been pursuing low volume, richer and but more exclusive tourist clientele environmental friendly tourism and quality tourism. These two policies are by their nature contradictory and it will be difficult to have a common tourism promotion strategy.

iii) There are different levels of infrastructure and superstructure development in the three Partner States. These differences imply that it will be difficult to have one common tourism policy.

iv)   The danger and risk of a common East African tourism industry is, however, that should anything happen in the expanded market (diseases, political turmoil, etc.) the entire market in East Africa will be affected.

What Should be Done First?

i)   Aim at harmonizing the tourism policies first.

ii) Harmonize the infrastructure in the three countries and the environmental impact on expanded tourism in Tanzania has to be properly assessed.

iii) Cooperation, particularly in tourism, has to aim at mutual benefit and equitable sharing of the benefits from tourism

iv) There should not be a rush into allowing free flow of tourists and tourist vehicles. If this is decided in a rush there will be negative repercussions on employment, particularly for Tanzanians employed by tour operators, etc.

v) Kenya should enter into joint venture arrangements with Tanzania to take advantage of the expanded tourism market.

vi) The issue of common East African passports needs to be critically examined in terms of the effects it will have on employment, especially in the tourism sector.

As noted at the beginning, in recent years Tanzanian tourism, like that of Uganda, has taken a tremendous leap forward. There was a 237.9 percentage change in receipts in Tanzania between 1991 and 1996 compared with 41% recorded in Kenya over the same period. In absolute terms during this period earnings increased from 95 to 238 US $ million and from 432 to 493 US $ million in Tanzania and Kenya respectively (Table 7.2 above).

On the other hand Uganda has the least earnings in absolute terms that is an increase of 15 US $ Million in 1991 to 82 US $ Mill in 1996. Actually Uganda did very well in relative terms increasing its earnings by 447 percent over the same period! While Tanzania need not relate all the measures it took to protect her tourist industry from competition with Kenya it must study all the options coolly. Uganda may be where the major competition will come from and Tanzania needs to study what Uganda is doing even more carefully!

CRITICAL ISSUES, PROBLEMS AND PROPOSED MEASURES

This chapter deals with issues, which are critical to the signing of the EAC Treaty and subsequent membership of Tanzania in the EAC. Issues, which appear under 12.1, are central to the whole discussion of the Treaty and Tanzania's membership in the EAC. Most of the views are drawn from stakeholders' interviews. Critical issues numbering 12.2 to 12.10 are sector specific. They are drawn from the analysis as well as from stakeholders' interviews.

CRITICAL ISSUES ON TANZANIA'S PREPAREDNESS FOR EAST AFRICAN COOPERATION

Issue 1: The Kind of EAC Tanzania Wants

Various stakeholders interviewed seem to suggest that Tanzania wants to see an *"equitable development of the Partner States"*. Specifically Tanzania wants to carry out the following:

a) To create conditions for rapid growth of exports.

b) To exploit opportunities for economies of scale in infrastructure *(transport and communications, energy) and services (financial institutions, education, health, water)* at regional level.

c) To support sustainable industrial development and economic diversification.

Issue 2: Conditions Leading to the Signing of the East African Treaty

During consultations a number of proposals were made. They include:

a) Identifying areas in the Treaty which make their implementation currently difficult and proposing appropriate changes.

b) Including the proposed amendments in the Treaty.

c) Collecting people's views on the East African Cooperation Treaty.

d) Signing the amended Treaty.

Issue 3: Necessary Measures that would lead Tanzania to Participate Effectively and Competitively in the East African Community

The measures are categorized into immediate, medium and long-term.

Immediate -Term Measures

Form an *East African Cooperation Preparedness Unit* to be known as *EAC Preparedness Unit*. The main focus of *EAC Preparedness Unit* should be to deal with questions, which the Government of Tanzania believes are crucial in improving the country's participation, overall performance and competitiveness in the EAC.

The secretariat of the EAC Preparedness Unit should be located in the Ministry of Foreign Affairs and International Cooperation but should have an advisory committee which includes members from key stakeholders in government, public sector and private sector (including research institutes) from the Mainland and Zanzibar.

The major issues which the *EAC Preparedness Unit* should focus on, among others, include:

a) Designing ways of increasing the quantity and quality of business investment in Tanzania;

b) Encouraging operating firms to have better performance and be competitive

c) Encouraging low performing firms to maximize their potential by adopting best practices; and

d) Improving the opportunities of both large and small businesses to exploit information technology.

In order to achieve the above outputs the following activities will have to be carried out by *EAC Preparedness Unit.*

a) Identify current and future constraints which impede the performance of businesses in Tanzania;

b) Prioritize the constraints for effective elimination;

c) Identify the major actors in resolving the constraints;

d) Agree on the roles of different partners (government, private sector, individuals, etc) in eliminating the constraints/bottlenecks;

e) Work out practical proposals on how to improve Tanzania's business competitiveness within and outside EAC. To implement this:

   i) Design a mechanism which would take account of the disadvantaged in order to raise their competitiveness;

   ii) Conduct the following studies, which would enhance the extent of Tanzania's participation and competitiveness:

   • A study on the capacity building situation (Tanzania Mainland and Zanzibar) and the potential impact of free movement of labour and capital to economic development;

   • A study on the opportunities of harmonizing the monetary and fiscal policies in the Tanzanian economy;

   • A study on the probable gains and losses of Tanzania's participation in EAC;

- A study on the effects of tariff reduction and how it can best be done.

iii) Make the East African Treaty, a *People-centred Economic Community* by collecting views from the private sector, civic organizations and other individual citizens.

The Medium-term Measures

i)   Identify key areas in which Tanzania has a comparative advantage or are of critical importance;
ii) Identify infant industries which need protection;
iii) Establish industrial benchmarks for tariff reduction eligibility; and
iv) Invest in capacity building (software and hardware).

The Long-term Measures

i)   Invest in capacity building (software and hardware);
ii)   Improve infrastructure and economic services; and
iiii) Improve productive sectors.

CRITICAL ISSUES ON TRADE

Issue 4: Insufficient Data Base

Problem: Tanzania is not in a position to monitor her participation and developments in the East African Cooperation due to an insufficient data base.

Recommendation: Tanzania should invest in capacity building and build a sufficient data base for quantifying her participation in the EAC.

Issue 5: Elimination of Import duties for Imports from Partner States (Zero Tariff Rate by July 31, 1999) and Agree on Common External Tariff

Problem

a) Significant government revenue loss from import duties if zero tariff rate is imposed by July 31, 1999 and its implications on Tanzania's cash budget system.

b) The formula of how the customs revenue would be shared is not known.
c) Loss of revenue arising from the use of cheaper imports if internal tariffs are eliminated while external tariffs differ among Partner States.

Recommendation: The elimination of import duties should be gradual, and there should be harmonization of external tariffs. The draft treaty for EAC needs to explicitly show the mechanism of sharing the customs revenue.

CRITICAL ISSUES ON AGRICULTURE

Issue 6: Low Productivity Levels in Agriculture

Problem: Current productivity in Tanzanian agriculture measured by cereal yields per hectare is lower than in the Partner States.

Recommendation: Cooperate with the Partner States in developing technologies and extension messages, which are relevant for the development of the agricultural sector.

Issue 7: Poor Rural Transport Network

Problem: The majority of rural people walk long distances to and from the markets and other service centres.

Recommendation: Develop rural road network for making the agricultural sector more dynamic and productive.

CRITICAL ISSUES ON INDUSTRY

Issue 8: Most Tanzanian Industries Cannot Survive in the Event of Competing With Similar Products From Partner States

Problem
a) The costs of production are too high caused by high utility costs, taxes and poor infrastructure;

b) lack of dynamic entrepreneurial sector.

Recommendations
a) Gradually reduce the protective rates for locally-produced products;

b) Seriously address the problem of infrastructure (roads, railways, air transport, telecommunications);

c) Invest in capacity building of entrepreneurial sector;

d) Diversify the industrial base;

e) Financial institutions should provide support to indigenous entrepreneurs through development and export finance; and

f) Study the impact of taxes on industrial competitiveness and performance.

Issue 9: Development of Small and Medium-scale Industries

Problem: Lack of concrete measures to facilitate small and medium-scale industries in Tanzania.

Recommendations
a) Clearly define a policy on small and medium-scale enterprises (SME);

b) Define strategy and specific actions to stimulate the development of the SME sector.

Issue 10: Harmonization and Rationalization of Investment Incentives

*Problem:*The quantitative investment incentives are not uniform in the three Partner States.

*Recommendation:*Each Partner State should improve the current incentives (tax holidays, lisencing procedures, financial infrastructure, etc.).

Issue 11: Cooperation in Standardization and Quality Assurance

Problem: Lack of comprehensive national policy on matters of quality, standardization and testing.

Recommendations
a) Strengthen the legal framework on these issues.

b) Accredit internationally the Tanzania Bureau of Standards so that her certificates are recognized worldwide.

CRITICAL ISSUES ON TRANSPORT

Issue 12:Economic Infrastructure

Problem: Poor Infrastructure in general.

Recommendations
a) Improve telecommunication services;

b) Increase the number and length of paved roads.

CRITICAL ISSUES ON TOURISM AND NATURAL RESOURCES

Issue 13: Common Tourism Promotion Policy/Strategy

Problems

a) Contradictory tourism strategies (high volume, mass tourism *vs* low volume environmentally friendly, quality tourism);

b) Different levels of infrastructure and superstructure of Partner States; and

c) Undefined formula for sharing equitably the revenue from tourism.

Recommendations
a) Harmonize the tourism policies first; and

b) Harmonize the development of infrastructure in the three Partner States.

4

LEGAL ANALYSIS OF THE DRAFT TREATY FOR THE ESTABLISHMENT OF THE EAST AFRICAN COMMUNITY

*Sengondo Mvungi**

TREATY MAKING IN INTERNATIONAL LAW

Treaty making is a sovereign act within the competence of states. It is a process in public international law through which states enter into binding contracts and agreements aimed at defining, providing for and sanctifying social, political, economic and cultural relations between them. The general law governing treaty-making is the Vienna Convention on the Law of Treaties, 1969.

If the arduous and complicated treaty-making process could be summarized, then major steps in treaty-making are:

- Pre-Treaty consultations and negotiations normally undertaken by officials of the treaty-making states;
- The signing of the treaty by Plenipotentiaries and/or head of states;
- Ratification; and
- Incorporation of the treaty in municipal law of State Parties to the treaty.

The present Draft Treaty for the establishment of a new East African Community is still at the 1st stage whereby consultations within and among the Partner States, namely Kenya, Uganda and Tanzania, are still going on. It is expected that this process will have come to an end in July 1999 when the Heads of States of the three Partner States are expected to sign the treaty instrument.

---

* Doctor of laws and Senior Lecturer at the Department of Constitutional and Administrative law

Perhaps the most novel aspect of the treaty-making process adopted by the three states, which aspect is normally ignored in treaty-making, is the importance of consulting the people in the domestic jurisdiction of the Partner States before the states conclude the treaty. The fact that the people of East Africa are being asked to give their opinion on the draft treaty is admittedly a break-through in the regional cooperation process. It means that leaders of East Africa have learnt from the failure of the former East African Community. Among the main reasons for that failure was lack of involvement and therefore support of the civil society within the East African States for the East African Community. The former East Africa Community was a Community of States rather than an organization or club of the people of East Africa. Decision making was bureaucratized and vested in institutions that were isolated and far removed from the people. The people of East Africa had no say in whatever took place in the East African Community. So its collapse, though regrettable, drew far too little sympathy from East Africans. It is also true that even if East Africans would have wished to rise up to the occasion in defence of the community, there was no forum through which they could channel their response.

ISSUES SURROUNDING THE DISSOLVED AFRICAN COMMUNITY

Background to the Collapse of the East African Community

In 1977 the East Africa Community was officially dissolved. This step, unfortunate though it was, was applauded in many circles within the three East African States. The majority of those who applauded the collapse of the EAC said it interfered with or narrowed their influence and activities within their nation states. The scope of their operations and vision for the future, whether economic or political, was limited to being a big fish in a small pond rather than vice versa. Such elements saw the opportunity for self-enhancement when the common services collapsed and were replaced by national and/or private concerns.

Some other circles, however, celebrated the collapse of the EAC for quite different reasons. The EAC had become an innefficient organization and was failing to deliver common services and to discharge its obligations. Deliberate refusal by state authorities to act in accordance with the treaty frustrated many well-intentioned EAC employees.

Be that as it may, the dissolution of the EAC marked a great failure in a long struggle of the people of Africa generally, and East Africa in particular, to achieve economic and social integration which remains a major factor in the process towards African Unity and the liberation of the African people from underdevelopment.

It is common ground that East African cooperation is a century-old theme. Although some historians have recorded its early beginnings in the establishment of British colonialism in East Africa, this is largely ahistorical, taking into account the socio-economic history of the region. The roots of cooperation in the East African region go beyond the colonization of East Africa. Before then, East Africa was a region in socio- economic and political flux, with various people groups, a trade route network, political dynamism and social mingling that had for centuries succeeded in establishing common cultural identity and a non-tribal a common language known as *Kiswahili*[1]. It was therefore not the colonization of East Africa, with the subsequent construction of the Uganda railway, that made it possible for the British to create a common services organization, first between Kenya and Uganda and later with Tanganyika.[2] Rather, it was the common identity, and socio-economic linkages within the East African communities that made it possible for Britain to establish the East African Common Services. As will be seen later, the British could not achieve any more integration of East Africa than the people in the region were ready to have. It should be mentioned that as early as 1899 the British were desirous of forging closer integration of the two East African Territories, Kenya and Uganda, under one political umbrella, to wit, an East African federation. Sir Harry Johnson, the British Special Commissioner to Uganda, was given instructions by the British Government to consider the merits of a closer cooperation between Kenya and Uganda in the form of an amalgamation and to locate a site for the federal capital.[3].

---

[1] Taasisi ya Ukuzaji wa Mitaala: Kiswahili kwa Sekondari, Dar es Salaam (1988)

[2] Tanganyika joined the East African Common Services Organization after the defeat of the Germans in the First World War that ended in 1918. In 1919, following the capitulation under the Treaty signed between Germany and the Allied Powers at Versailles, Tanganyika was placed under British rule as a mandate Territory by the League of Nations. Article 10 of the British Mandate Agreement for Tanganyika, 1920, gave Britain the powers to asssociate Tanganyika to certain administrative, customs and fiscal arrangements with her adjacent neighbours under British rule, provided that this did not infringe the Mandate.

Although Johnston recommended amalgamation, the support his proposals received in the Colonial Office was not strong enough to have his plans implemented. Some writers believe that the completion of the Kenya-Uganda railway and the establishment of a common Railways Authority between the two territories made Johnston's proposals unnecessary.[4]

The institutionalization of the East Africa cooperation under British colonialism rule therefore with the establishment of a common railway administration between Kenya and Uganda in 1902. In 1905 an East African Currency Board was established between Kenya and Uganda. In 1911 the two countries established a common Postal Union and in 1917 they established a Customs Union. Tanganyika joined the Currency Board in 1921, then the Customs Union in 1923 and finally the Postal Union in 1933.[5] European Settlers in Kenya were very much in favour of a federation, so they made an appeal for amalgamation in 1905 which received considerable support from Sir Percy Girouard the man who became the Governor of the East African Protectorate in 1909. The Colonial Foreign Office was however hesitant about these proposals.[6] The actual problem was that an East African federation as demanded by the White Settlers meant the establishment of a self-governing White only Colony in East Africa in which African interests played no part at all.[7] The debate on the East African Federation came up again after the end of the First World War. As a consequence of this war, the allied Powers who had won forced Germany to sign a capitulation Treaty at Versailles in 1919 in which Germany renounced his suzerainty over its overseas territories. Tanganyika, then Deutsch-Oestafrika, was mandated to the British after breaking away from Burundi and Rwanda, these two territories being given to the Belgians. The British cautiously carried on with their desire to create an East African Federation mainly because of the legal diversity of their territorial possessions in East Africa. Originally, it was not possible to

---

[3] Igham, K., *Uganda's Old Eastern Province: The Transfer to East Africa Protectorate in 1902*, in *Uganda Journal* (March 1957) pp. 41-46, Oliver, R., *Sir Henry Johnson and the Scramble for Africa*, (1957), p. 336, 334 -335.

[4] Rosberg/Segal, *An East African Federation,* In the International Conciliation, no. 543, May 1963, p.11.

[5] Doimi di Delupis, I., The East African Community and Common Market, (1970) pp.19-20.

[6] Rosberg/Segal., An East African Federation, op. cit.pp. 11-12.

[7] Ibid. p. 14

treat the Ugandan Protectorate in the same way as the Kenyan Colony, and later it became even more difficult to resolve the legal differences when Tanganyika became a British mandate territory.

According to the Mandate Agreement, Britain could not do whatever it wanted with Tanganyika, since the legal title to the territory was vested in the League of Nations. The Mandate Agreement allowed Britain to associate Tanganyika with its neighbours under her possession only as far as it did not prejudice the status of the territory and infringe the interests of the Natives of the Territory.[8] Apparently, the demand for an East African Federation was being sought not by the Natives of the three territories but by the White Settlers who wanted to establish a white dominion of a self-governing status spreading from Kenya to Rhodesia.[9] The structure of the self-governing "White dominion" was already taking shape in Kenya where the White Settlers had alienated the best arable lands which they then called "White Highlands", and restricted the Natives to infertile land which they called "Native Reserves". Africans were prohibited from entering the "White Highlands" unless with work permits given to migrant labourers. Furthermore, Africans were not included in government business as was exemplified by the total domination of the Kenyan Legislative Council by the White Settlers.[10]

The Colonial Office, acting under pressure from the White Settlers in Kenya, appointed a Parliamentary Commission under Ormsby-Gore who visited the three East African territories to see measures that were to be taken to accelerate the general economic development of the East African dependencies.[11] This Commission found that East Africans were not prepared for a federation, and that some quarters were openly hostile to this idea.[12] One of the major critics of the federation was the Tanganyika Governor Sir Donald Cameroon, who saw the total subjugation of native interests in Kenya and Uganda as a recipe for bad government in Tanganyika, which was a Mandated Territory.[13]

The idea of an East African Federation came up again when the Colonial Office was forced to appoint another parliamentary inquiry headed by

---

[8] Article 10 of the Mandate Agreement Drawn by the Supreme Council of Peace Conference and Approved for the League
[9] Rosberg/Segal., *An East African Federation*, op.cit.p. 14
[10] Rosberg/Segal., ibid, p.14
[11] See: Cmnd. 2387, London, 1925
[12] ibid
[13] Rosberg/Segal., *An East African Federation,* op.cit.p. 14

Hiltonyoung between 1928 -29 to consider whether "either by federation or some other form of closer union, more effective cooperation between the different Governments in Central and Eastern Africa may be secured".[14] The Young Commission recommended closer cooperation and further institutionalization of the common services between the three territories of Kenya, Tanganyika and Uganda but argued that time was not ripe for such a drastic measure in the form of a federation. It suggested that the Central African territories should have another arrangement from that of East Africa.[15] The Young Commission Report was not wholly accepted by the Colonial Office and all attempts made by Sir Samuel Wilson, the Permanent Under Secretary to the Colonial Office, to doctor it failed to produce the required results.[16] Even the Joint Parliamentary Committee that was established to resolve the differences found that there were so many contradictions and differences that it was better to separate East Africa from the Central African territories and to let East Africa proceed alone in its path towards establishment of common services.[17]

As a result of this resolution, the East African Cooperation continued under the umbrella of the East African Governor's Conference, and some policies taken for one territory finally found acceptance with the Authorities of the other East African territories. For instance, when Kenya introduced income tax in 1937 to remedy her bad financial situation, this was extended to Tanganyika and Uganda in 1940. In the same year a Joint Income Tax Board was established to handle the collection of tax. A secretariat of the Governor's Conference finally took permanent form and a Joint Economic Council was established to liaise between the Common Services and the Civil Services of the three territories.[18]

Many of the Joint institutions established during the Second World War, like the East African Production and Supply Board and the Industrial Management Board, were mainly aimed at mobilizing material support for the British war effort, although their significance outlived the war. The change of the status of Tanganyika from a Mandate to a Trusteeship Territory by the

---

[14] Cmnd. 3234, London, 1929
[15] ibid.
[16] ibid. col. 263/A2.
[17] ibid.
[18] Ingham, K., *A History of East Africa*, (1963) pp. 315-375 and Doimi di Delupis, I.,*The East African Community and the Common Market*, op. cit. pp. 23-24

United Nations made it more difficult for Britain to integrate Tanganyika into an East African Federation that was mainly dominated by White Settlers. Article 5 of the Trusteeship Agreement provided, *inter alia*, that:

> "...the Administering Authority ... shall be entitled to constitute Tanganyika into a customs, fiscal, or administrative union or federation with adjacent territories under His Britannic Majesty's sovereignty or control, and to establish common services between such territories and Tanganyika where such measures are not inconsistent with the basic objectives of the international Trusteeship System and with the terms of this Agreement."

A Political federation of the type demanded by the Kenyan Settlers would obviously have infringed the terms of the Trusteeship Agreement. A White Settler-dominated political federation would completely infringe the interests of the Natives in Tanganyika whose objective was to attain independent statehood as a majority-ruled African State.[19] Therefore Britain chose to consolidate and exploit the economic rather than political potential of the territories by establishing in 1948 an East African High Commission, that would be a body corporate with supra-territorial competence to administer the Common Services and institutions spanning the three East African territories.[20]

The East African High Commission was not an international organisation, since Tanganyika, Kenya and Uganda were not States but territorial units under colonial and/or foreign occupation and rule. The Order-in-Council that established the High Commission was not a treaty, but just subsidiary legislation made by the Crown in England under the Foreign Jurisdiction Act of England. Although the proposal to establish the High Commission is said to have been accepted by the legislatures of the three territories, this was important only for the consumption of the British Parliament since for the people of the territories, the colonial legislative organs were not legitimate law-making organs. They were constituted by appointees of the Governor instead of elected representatives of the people and had no actual legislative powers since as dependencies, Tanganyika, Uganda and Kenya were under the legislative jurisdiction of the British Parliament.

---

[19] See also the provisions of the Trusteeship System, Articles 75 and 77 of the United Nations Charter.

[20] Colonial Paper no. 191 and Igham., *A History of East Africa,* op. cit.p. 401 and The East African (High Commision) Order-in-Council, 1947

The Order-in-Council establishing the East African High Commission came into force on the 1st day of January 1948. The High Commission was to be chaired by the Governor of Kenya and the Governors of Tanganyika and Uganda were to be members of this Commission. There was also established a Legislative Assembly presided over by a Speaker consisting of 7 *ex-officio* members who were officers of the Commission, one official member nominated by the Governor of each Territory, 13 Unofficial members, one member elected by the unofficial members of the legislative Councils (LEGCOs) in each territory, one African and one Indian member appointed by the Governor of each territory, and one Arab member elected/ appointed by the High Commission.[21] The Legislative Assembly had powers to make directly applicable laws in the jurisdictions of the three territories in all matters listed in the Order-in-Council, but the High Commission had powers either to veto, scrutinize and allow the legislation so made. Furthermore, the High Commission could, with consent, advise in all matters listed in the Order-in-Council provided that this was deemed to be expedient and in the interest of public order, public faith and good government. The High Commission could also legislate upon advice by the legislatures of the three territories.[22] The East African High Commission was successful in its implementation of its objectives and by the time the three East African territories approached independence, the services rendered by the High Commission were enormous. Despite the success, the High Commission remained an instrument of colonial domination and exploitation and the concentration of most of the High Commission's activities in Kenya became

---

[21] See. The East African (High Commission) Order-in-Council, 1947 in the Report of the High Commission, 1949 pp.4-5

[22] ibid. 18 items were listed in the Order-in-Council as areas of legislative comepetence of the Legislative Assembly. These include: appropriations providing for the expenditures of the High Commission and the common services, civil aviation, customs and excise excluding tariffs, income tax exluding tax rates and allowances, Lake Victoria fisheries, Makerere College (effective from 1st August 1948), metorological services, pensions and emoluments of service staff, posts, telegraphs and radio communication, railways, harbours and inland water transport (effective from 1st May 1948), loan ordinance for self-contained services, statistics and census, Royal Technical College (effective from 1949), merchant shipping (effective from 1949), peace, public order and good government in the three territories.

a bone of contention in the post-independence period that finally led to the collapse of the regional cooperation.[23]

Post-independence Period

As Tanganyika was about to become independent, it became necessary to make arrangements for the future of the High Commission post independence. In June 1961, delegations from the United Kingdom, Kenya, Uganda, Tanganyika and an observer from Zanzibar assembled in London to deliberate on the future of the High Commission. They agreed to preserve the activities of the High Commission under a restructured organisational framework taking into account the impending achievement of statehood and independence of the three territories. The High Commission was to be replaced by an East African Authority consisting of the Governors of Kenya and Uganda and the President of Tanganyika.[24] The new organisation was named the East African Common Services Organization (EASCO). Later the agreement was amended to include the Presidents of Kenya and Uganda when the two became independent.[25] The EASCO was a great improvement on the East African High Commission. It created five Ministerial Committees working directly under the Authority, in the fields of communication, finance, commercial and industrial cooperation, social and research services, and labour. Furthermore, the EASCO Agreement established an East African Court of Appeal to hear appeals from the High Courts of the three states. The EASCO could enter into agreement with the United Kingdom under which the East African Court of Appeal could hear cases of other territories, such as Aden, St. Helena, Seychelles and Somaliland.[26] This transferred the powers of the Privy Council to hear appeals from the three territories to the Court of Appeal of East Africa.

The powers of the East African Legislative Assembly were increased so that it could legislate not only on the 27 matters listed in the Annex to the EASCO Constitution, but could also legislate on its own powers usually referred to in German jurisprudence as *Kompetenzkompetenz*).[27] Contrary

---

[23] For a detailed explanation of the work of the Commission see: Doimi di Delupis, I., *The East African Community and Common Market*, op. cit. pp. 34-40

[24] Comnd. no. 1433, 1961 and no. 1279 of 1961

[25] Uganda became independent on 9th October 1962, and Kenya on 12 December 1963. Zanzibar was included in EASCO by Amendment no. 2 the EASCO agreement, 1964.

[26] EASCO Constitution Article 33

[27] ibid. item no. 7 in the list annexed to the EASCO Constitution states that the Legislative Assembly can legislate on "powers, privileges and immunities of the East African Legislative Assembly and the Chairman and the members thereof."

to the powers enjoyed by the European Union, where extension of the legislative powers of the Community can only be implied by way of construction to cover "any action which appears to be necessary for the functioning of the Organisation,"[28] Knowledge it is common ground that the EASCO managed to establish itself as a very competent regional integration organization with unprecedented supra-national powers. The free movement of goods, services, persons and capital was guaranteed, with a single currency ensuring a stable financial market without convertibility impediments. Although the internal institutional and investment imbalances in the East African Common market as a result of the colonial policies began to bear weight on the EASCO affairs, these were immediately palliated by the radical movement towards an East African Federation which the political leadership of the three territories were offering. When talks on the East African Federation began, it immediately became evident that Tanganyika was becoming independent on December 9th 1961. Nyerere, the leader of Tanganyika, offered to postpone the independence of Tanganyika by a year to facilitate the possibility of the three territories becoming independent as one single state. The leaders of Kenya and Uganda did not accept this offer, but rather opted for separate independence and gradual movement towards the East African Federation.

On the 5th June 1963, the leaders of the three territories issued the Nairobi Declaration committing their governments to a federal set-up within a year. Britain was called upon to grant independence to Kenya immediately to facilitate the East African Federation.[29] The three Leaders, Mr. Milton Obote of Uganda, Julius Nyerere of Tanganyika and Jomo Kenyatta of Kenya established a Working Party to prepare the Draft Constitution of the East African Federation, with instructions to submit a report within six weeks when a full constitutional conference was to be held to consider the proposals.[30] The Constitutional Conference never took place. Immediately after the appointment of the Working Party, Uganda began presenting hurdles that reduced the whole exercise to ashes. The bone of contention was on the sovereignty of Buganda which was an autonomous part of Uganda, coupled with the refusal of Uganda to surrender foreign affairs and citizenship to

---

[28] See the Case of Fe' dechar Recueil, II, pp. 201
[29] Rothchild, D., Politics of Intergration, op. cit. pp. 77-78
[30] Nairobi Declaration, of 5th June, 1963

the Federation.[31] Kenya and Tanganyika were of the opinion that these competencies belonged to the Federation. Disagreement on this issue put an end to the attempt to establish an East African Federation[32]

The failure to establish an East African Federation led to a re-negotiation of the structure of the East African Common Services Organization. The Differences that were suppressed by Partner States in order to facilitate the establishment of the Federation remained and were allowed to take their toll on the common regional organization. The imbalances of the economic structure of East Africa made Kenya the dominant partner while Tanganyika and Uganda played peripheral roles. After the failure to achieve an East African Federation, Tanganyika entered a treaty of Union with Zanzibar and became the United Republic of Tanzania on the 26th April, 1964. On 10th June, 1965 the East African states simultaneously announced the introduction of separate national currencies and the dissolution of the East African Currency Board. This decision was defended by both the International Monetary Fund and the members States, that in view of the failure of the Federation, the introduction of national currencies was in the national interest.[33]

---

[31] See: Motion on the Federation by the leader of the opposition Mr. Batariganya, *National Assembly Debates (Uganda) Official Report, Second Series*, Vo. 14 July, 5 1963 pp. 858-864, "Kabaka not at a Conference" a newspaper report Uganda Argus (Kampala) July, 1, 1963 p. 3 explaining the failure of the King of Uganda to attend the meeting by East African Federation; "No Federation this Year, but there is no need to Hurry", a statement by Adoko Nekyon, Ugandan Minister for Information, Broadcasting and Tourism stating why Uganda will not hurry to join the East African Federation in Uganda Argus (Kampala) August 21 1963, and "Uganda view on Federation - points must be Settled" a statement by the Leader of Uganda Mr. Milton Obbote in East African *Standard* (Nairobi) Octobber 8, 1963 p.1

[32] For details on the Kenyan position see: Motion by the leader of the Opposition Mr. Ronald Ngala on the East African Federation, in *House of Representatives Debates (Kenya) Official Report*, First Session, Vol. 1 (June 27 1963), and for details on Tanganyika's position see: *National Assembly Debates (Tanganyika Official Report*, Seventh Meeting (June 20, 1963 Cols. 696-698, and *Report on Meetings and Dicussions on the Proposed East African Federation*, Information Services of Tanganyika and Zanzibar, (Dar es Salaam) 1964

[33] For the Kenyan statement on separate currencies see: *House of Representatives Debates, Official Report*, Second Session Vol V. 1965 Col283, on Tanzanian position see: *The Nationalist*, 14 June 1965 p. 3, and Nyerere's Speech to the Parliament reported in the Nationalist 14 June, 1966p.7;on Uganda's position see: *National Assembly Debates (Uganda) Official Report*, Second Series. Vol47 (June 10, 1965) pp.2165-2166; see also van Arkadie., Federation in East Africa, Nairobi 1965 pp. 152 et seq,; Green/ Krishna., *Economic Cooperation in Africa*, Nairobi, 1967 p. 35

Tanzania came up with two arguments, namely, that it had accepted the EASCO arrangement on the basis that East African Federation would be achieved in the near future but that having failed it was only natural as a sovereign state to control its own monetary affairs; secondly, that an East African central banking system could only be achieved by devolution of powers to individual states to establish cooperation between independent national banks rather than through a single centrally-controlled central bank. The argument here was that the latter would be fraught with controversies and misunderstandings that would only help to strain the relations between the three Partner States.[34]

It is argued that for the smooth running of a Common Market, a single currency was an important advantage in ensuring the free movement of goods, capital, services and persons. The problem with the investment structure of the economies of the East African States was that most production-oriented investments and service institutions were concentrated in Kenya. Since Tanzania and Uganda had little to offer as goods in the common market, the continuation of the single currency would be more to the advantage of Kenya than the two weaker partners. Although in the short run Tanzania's position was correct, taking a long-term perspective on the changing nature of investment patterns in any free market-led economy, and taking into account the need to maintain the common services and the common-market, what EASCO should have done was to work on a proper monetary policy ensuring proper control of the financial market and market share benefits to the weaker economic partners than dissolving the Common Currency Board.

Following the dissolution of the East African Currency Board, some Member States began introducing measures aimed at individual rectification of the existing imbalances in the economic structure of the EASCO by introducing certain restrictions to trade.[35] This led to immediate reactions in the Common Services and a commission was appointed under Professor Kjeld Phillip of Denmark to study the problems facing the EASCO. Professor Phillip submitted his Report which made proposals for restructuring the EASCO into an economic Community.[36] These proposals were accepted and the East African Community was established by a Treaty signed by the heads of State of Tanzania, Kenya and Uganda on the 6th June, 1967. The Treaty came into force on 1st December, 1967[37]

---

[34] See: *The Nationalist,* (Dar es Salaam) June 14, 1965 p. 3
[35] According to Deimi di Delupis, it is Tanzania that began taking such measures. See: *East African Community and Common Market,* op. cit.p. 51
[36] Deimi di Delupis, I., *The East African Community and Common Market,* op. cit.p. 51

The major aims of the East African Community were economic cooperation and development. The Treaty provided for strengthening and regulation of industrial and other commercial relations among the Partner States with a view to promoting harmonious and balanced development and equitable sharing of benefits[38] In order to achieve this objective, the Member States undertook to ensure the existence of: common tariffs and excise duties, abolition of quantitative restrictions to trade between the Partner States, establishment of a common agricultural policy, creation of an East African Development Bank, retention of current account of payments between Partner States, harmonization of monetary policies and consultations necessary for the maintenance of the common market, continuation of common services, proximation of commercial law and coordination of economic planning and transport policies.[39]

The Treaty established the following organs or institutions: The East African Authority, the East African Legislative Assembly, the East African Ministers, The East African Community Councils and the Common Market Tribunal[40] The East African Authority was the highest decision-making, supervisory and controlling organ of the Community, consisting of the Heads of State of the Three Partner States[41] The Authority was immediately assisted by the East African Ministers, who were appointees of the Heads of the State of the Three Partner States, provided that, in appointing an East African Minister, the appointing Authority shall ensure that his appointee is a person qualified as a voter in the electoral laws of his country and is not immediately a member of his country's cabinet[42] The latter proviso was included in order to ensure that an East African Minister is independent from national politics of his country.

The East African Ministers were the actual political functionaries of the Community, responsible for running its day-to-day affairs, and were members of every council established by the Treaty.[43] They were directly accountable to the Authority and their tenure of service was determined by the Authority.[44] The Treaty establishing the East African Community did away with the

---

[37] Treaty of the East African Community, 1967 Article 91
[38] ibid. Article 2 (1)
[39] ibid. Article 2 (2)
[40] ibid. Article 3
[41] ibid. Articles 46, 47 and 48.
[42] ibid. Article 49
[43] ibid. Articles 51 and 54
[44] ibid. Article 50

Committee System employed by EASCO and introduced a councils system instead. The five councils established by the Treaty were: the Common Market Council, the Communications Council, the Economic Consultative and Planning Council, the Finance Council and the Research and Social Council.[45] Except for the Communications Council and the Finance Council, which had only six members, namely, the three East African Ministers and three other National Ministers from the each Member State, the other three councils had twelve members of whom three were the East African Ministers and three National Ministers. [46] The functions of each Council were set out in the Treaty and these included the carrying out of the specific duties and functions stipulated in the Treaty in their field or area. [47]

The EAC Treaty established the East African legislative Assembly (EALA) in the same way and with similar powers as had been in the EASCO Agreement. The Legislative Assembly was composed of three east African ministers, their deputies (if any), twenty seven appointed members, a Chairman of the Assembly, the Secretary General of the Community and the counsel to the Community. [48] Other than the changes in the composition of the Assembly the actual method of recruitment of members of the Assembly remained appointive, rather than elective. This left the Community in the same situation of isolation and alienation from the mainstream of communal or grassroots politics as was the case with its predecessor the EASCO. The member states had equal representation in the Assembly, to wit, one East African Minister, his deputy (if any), and nine appointed members. The tenure of the legislature was perpetual, but the members of the Assembly served until the legislative period of the Government that appointed them met after it was next dissolved.[49]

The East African Legislative Assembly was vested with powers of enacting laws of the Community in the areas of Community jurisdiction. The Acts of the EALA were effected by means of Bills passed and assented by each member of the Authority. Any Act so passed and assented became directly enforceable law in the domestic jurisdiction of the Partner States, but the members of the Authority jointly or severally had powers to withhold assent [50] If withholding of assent persisted for more than 9 months, such an Act lapsed. [51]

---

[45] ibid. Article 53
[46] ibid. Article 54
[47] ibid. Article 55
[48] ibid. Article 56
[49] ibid. Article 58
[50] ibid. Articles 59 and 60
[51] ibid. Article 60(2)

The EAC Treaty provided for an elaborate staffing system of the institutions of the Community. The Secretary General was the chief executive officer in the services of the Community. He was assisted by a counsel to the Community and an Auditor General.[52] The Treaty provided for an East African Community Service Commission whose members were appointed by the Authority from time to time in such numbers as the Authority deemed fit. The members of the Service Commission were to be highly qualified persons eligible to hold the post of Minister, Deputy Minister, a parliamentary secretary or member of the parliament in the legislature of the Partner States. The Commission had the responsibility of making appointments, transfers, promotions and disciplining of the staff of the Community and its institutions with the exception of members of the Common Market Tribunal and the Court of Appeal of East Africa.[53]

The Treaty establishing the EAC provided also for a two-tier dispute settlement mechanism, namely, the Court System and the Tribunal system.[54] The Court System consisted of an apex court, namely, the Court of Appeal for East Africa as had been established in the EASCO Agreement [55] The jurisdiction of the Court of Appeal for East Africa was to hear appeal cases from the High Courts of the three Partner States as provided for by the laws of each Partner State.[56] This clearly created an apex court with roots in the domestic legal system of the Partner States. The impact of such a system was to make the work of proximation of laws in East Africa easier, since all the Partner States adhere to Common law tradition especially with regard to the doctrines of precedent and *Stare decisis*.

The Tribunal system included the East African Industrial Court.[57] established by Article 84 of the EAC Treaty to deal with pensions and trade disputes, and the Common Market Tribunal established by Article 32 of the EAC Treaty to deal with disputes arising from the Common Market established and provided for in Chapter II to IX of the EAC Treaty. The Treaty decentralized the location of the institutions of the Community so that there was a balance of interests and multiplier effect of Community

---

[52] ibid. Article 61
[53] ibid. Articfles 62, 63 and 64
[54] ibid, Articles 80 and 81
[55] ibid. Article 80 and 85
[56] ibid. Article 80
[57] ibid. Article 81

affairs. Thus the Headquarters of the Community, the tribunal, secretariat and the East African Harbours were located in Tanzania, the East African Development Bank and the East African Posts and Telecommunications were located in Uganda, and the East African Railways and Airways were located in Kenya.[58]

Some observers have commented that the most significant aspect of the Treaty that established the East African Community was the placing together of the common services inherited from EASCO and until then the informal Common Market. Thus the informal Common Market acquired legal foundation.[59] The fact that this achievement was a formal one is not necessarily reflective of the organisational effectiveness of the EAC. The real test of the latter was the readiness of the Member States to implement measures establishing the Common Market. These measures were of two types, namely, actions aimed at the distribution of industrial projects to be sponsored by the Community through its Development Bank [60] and transfer tax levied on goods of a Member State to the extent where by the Member State has a trade balance against the weaker trading Partners.[61] These measures were believed to be the solution for the industrial and trade imbalance that existed in Tanzania and Uganda vis-á-vis Kenya.

It has been observed that the first three years of the Community were so successful that the neighbouring States began showing interest and seeking membership of the Community.[62] This apparent success was however short lived because soon national considerations (and sometimes selfish personal interests camouflaged as issues of national interest or sovereignty) and actual political instability in the member States began haunting the Community. The event that finally led to the collapse of the Community was the overthrow of the civilian government of Dr. Milton Obote of Uganda by a military junta led by General Iddi Amin on January 25, 1971. Obote fled to Tanzania where he enjoyed the friendship of the then Tanzania President, Julius

---

[58] ibid. Article 84
[59] ibid. Articles 86 and 87
[60] Pothlom/Friedland (eds)., *Integration and tegration in East Africa*, University Press of America, Brunswick, Maine 1980 at p. 19
[61] Treaaty Establishing the East African Community, Article 21 and Article 1 (b) of the Charter Establishing the East African Development Bank.
[62] ibid. Article 20

Nyerere. The refusal of Tanzania to recognise the Government of Iddi Amin meant that the consensus needed to enact Community law disappeared.

Further, the East African Authority could not meet since Nyerere refused to do any business with Amin. Perhaps things would have slowly evened up if Amin had played the gentleman. On the contrary, the unfortunate General maintained a constant war of words with Nyerere, trying to force him to expel Obote from Tanzania if Nyerere wanted to get the cooperation of Uganda on East African Community affairs.[63] Perhaps the most difficult moment in the affairs of the Community was when Amin unleashed a reign of terror in Uganda, beginning with nationalization of businesses belonging to Asians and their expulsion *à la* Adolf Hitler, to the extermination of prominent Ugandans suspected of being critical of his reign. In such a situation, the relationship with Uganda became difficult to maintain. In the meantime it is said that Tanzania and Uganda began withholding cash remittances to the headquarters of the East African Railways.[64] For many reasons the relationships between Tanzania and Kenya deteriorated, just as those between Kenya and Uganda. In fact, for all intents and purposes, the Community had ceased to exist, except only on paper, and bureaucrats in each Partner State were already considering fall back measures to be taken when the inevitable finally happened.

Decisions were already being taken by certain Corporations to prevent funds being transferred to the head offices, creating serious problems that eventually led to the collapse of the Community. The last blow was delivered by the decision of the East African Airways to suspend less profitable routes, namely, routes serving the weaker Partner States, Tanzania and Uganda, and the order by the Kenyan Government grounding of the East African Airways and establishing in its place a national Airline, brought the Community to its final demise. The decision to suspend certain less profitable routes interfered with interests of the weaker Member States, Uganda and Tanzania, while the grounding of the East African Airways and the establishment of Kenya Airways amounted to a total breach of the Treaty.

---

[63] Potholm/Fredland (eds)., *Integration and Disintegration in East Africa*, op. city. 23, and Doimi di Delupis, I., *The East African Community and Common Market*, op. cit. pp. 125-128. According to Doimi, Zambia applied for membebrship the same day the Community was established on 1st December 1967, and later Ethiopia and Somalia also applied to join. (pp.1260-27)

[64] East African Standard, Feb. 7. 1973.

The other Partner States reacted in panic, closing borders, and freezing Community assets. The East African Community had ceased to exist.

The problem that perplexes all observers is how such a formidable regional integration arrangement could have failed. Efforts that were being made to revive the Community date back to 30th November 1993 when the Agreement on East African cooperation was signed by the Heads of States of Tanzania, Uganda and Kenya[65]. These efforts are interesting but unrealizable if the very causes of failure to achieve, firstly, the Federation and later economic cooperation through a Community are glossed over and left unsolved. It is possible to see through the very political acts of reviving the East African Community as an act of self-preservation by the political leadership in East Africa when faced with serious internal problems. It would seem each member state wants the Community for its own selfish reasons. We need not go into this subject in this study but what we must bear in mind is that the people of East Africa need not be dragged into unworkable regional integration arrangements any more.

As far as Tanzania is concerned, the present efforts to revive the East African Community make no sense at the moment when there are already in place two competing regional integration arrangements, namely the SADC and COMESA of which she is a member. It is a fact that Kenya and Uganda are members of COMESA but have not yet joined the SADC. If Kenya and Uganda became SADC members today, would they still wish to have an East African cooperation? Perhapes yes. If this assumption is true, then an East African cooperation that will survive despite the existence and operation of SADC and COMESA must have solid foundations. It must offer East Africans something more than the two competing regional integration arrangements are offering. The only new product that makes the new East African Cooperation special is its commitment to the East African Federation, the very basic goal that its predecessors failed to achieve. If this is accepted as the basic denominator, then we can conclude that the new EAC will survive and finally achieve the objective that has always been the dream of the people of East Africa. Tanzania should not withdraw from this noble endeavour.

---

[65] Tanzania Information: *Tansania/Kenia/Uganda. Vetrage uber neueliche enge Zusammenarbeit*, 01/1994 January, p.1

From the foregoing discussion the following conclusions emerge:

1. That East Africa Cooperation is an age old aspiration of the people of East Africa.

2. That the Colonial Power that ruled East African States was not the originator of the East Africa Cooperation as some Euro-centric historians would wish to depict.

3. That the failure of the post independence governments to forge political Union was regrettable and a set-back in the struggle of the East African people to create a new identity for themselves and to lay the foundation for their economic and social emancipation.

4. That the failure by the dissolved East African Community to involve the people of East Africa in the Community affairs, the continued disproportionate sharing of benefits of the Community among member states, lack of adequate policies to resolve those weaknesses and conflicts were major factors that led to the collapse of the former EAC.

5. That as long as political federation is the final goal of the new EAC, the new EAC must learn from this failure and avoid the creation of a similar institution that will inevitably collapse.

Post -EAC Developments

The establishment of the new EAC cannot be done outside the context of the developments that have taken place ever since the collapse of the old EAC. The major developments that need to be addressed are as follows:

i)   Growth and consolidation of narrow national identity even though such identity is not matched with credible economic performance.

ii) Establishment of competing and overlapping regional integration arrangements, i.e. COMESA and SADC of which most EA states are members.

iii) Political liberalization/democratization that has created different political standards among member states.

iv) Breakout of war and/or inter-state conflicts among or involving members of the East African Cooperation.

We deal briefly with each of these developments in turn.

Growth of Narrow National Identity

It is now almost 40 years since the three East African states won their independence. The failure in 1963 to establish a political federation led to the phasing out of the East African Common Services Organization and the East African Currency Board.

The East African Community established to take over EASCO was an agreement to disagree rather than a feasible economic community. The political will having disappeared, integration efforts came under constant pressure. The community finally collapsed as a consequence of narrow nationalism that has grown and consolidated itself to date.

The economic miracles that the selfish individuals who pushed the community to collapse anticipated have never materialized in any of the East African States. The three countries are hamstrung with debt burdens and their growth rates are minimal. Yet if the new community is to survive, the narrow nationalism in the three states has to be dealt with. The community must make efforts to develop a new East African identity. In order to achieve this, the community must immediately after its inauguration establish programmes that directly involve individual East Africans so that the community anchors itself in the Civil Society rather than remain a bureaucratic institution among East African States.

Competing Integration Arrangement

It is common ground that COMESA and SADC represent hurdles in the realization of East African integration. To make sense the new East African Community must have something new to offer its members that is not being offered by the two competing integration arrangements. It has been suggested that the political objectives of a federation make the EAC a sensible undertaking. For this reason therefore the new EAC Treaty must aim at maximizing political dividends. These are easily achievable and make greater impact n the politics of integration. It is suggested that the element of political will should not be underplayed. Maximum benefits must be reaped from its interplay in community affairs. State leaders of the three Partner States should increasingly surrender political sovereignty to the community so as to achieve the federation in the shortest time possible. The attempt to retain veto powers over community legislation is a counter productive measure that makes the future community a non-starter.

Political Liberalizations

It is understood that not all Partner States have achieved similar standards in the field of political liberalisation. Plural democracy is still in its infancy in Kenya and Tanzania. In Uganda the dominant political system is still monolithic, i.e. no party system. It may take time until the same standards of democratization are achieved in each member state. Efforts should however be made to put pressure on them achieve in the shortest time possible the commonly accepted standards of good governance, democracy, human rights and the elimination of corruption.

War and Conflicts

Amongst the three Partner States, Uganda is still faced with internal rebellion. This may be resolved if the community takes faster and broader democratization measures. The involvement of Uganda in DRC problems complicates further her problems. Internal strife in Kenya and Tanzania has been largely resolved by tolerance and commitment to democratisation process. But Kenya should be advised to put an end to tribalism as an essential form of political governance. Tribalism is a divisive rather than an integrative factor in East African politics.

It has also been proposed that Rwanda and Burundi be admitted as members of the community. This proposal is premature. These states are too unstable and war-torn to be viable members of the new community. In any event it should be a principle that countries that have not achieved equivalent standards of peace, tranquillity and democratization should not be admitted as members of the Community.

THE DRAFT TREATY FOR THE ESTABLISHMENT OF A NEW EAST AFRICAN COMMUNITY

The Character of the New East African Community

The discussion on the Draft Treaty for the establishment of new East African Community must always bear in mind one fact, namely, that by establishing the East African Community, East Africans are not inventing the wheel. Regional integration is a global trend that has been in existence for more than a century. The people of East Africa are in possession of valuable experience in regional integration matters through their membership in several competing regional integration arrangements.

The discussion on the Draft Treaty has to take off based on a clear understanding of the nature or character of the new community as distinct from the former dissolved community and other competing regional integration arrangements. One has to be able to answer two questions, namely:

a) What is new in the proposed treaty?

b) What benefits are member states expected to enjoy?

But before we can answer these and other questions, it is important to state certain theoretical points of departure from which the discussion shall be made. The first is the definition of the term "integration". It is generally accepted that the term integration may have many meanings but, for the purposes of this study, it shall mean a constituent process through which new regional supra-national entities or organizations are created by bringing together two or more states and their subjects in an associative or cooperative arrangement in order to achieve common purposes or objectives that would otherwise remain unachievable had each state acted alone.[66] This broad definition covers all sorts of regional integration arrangements regardless of their nature or character. The latter depends on whether a particular regional integration arrangement is associative or cooperative in its genesis. In international relations institutionalization of cooperation results in bilateral and multilateral arrangements and institutions of universal character aimed at undertaking common tasks without necessarily compromising the sovereign character of the cooperating Partner States.

However, where states enter into supra-national association amongst themselves, they are entering into a constitutive process aimed at political Union. This implies that such states are not aiming at cooperation alone. They are interested in creating an organization that will finally supersede them and become a regional state.

In such cases their establishing instruments are *sui generis* aimed at providing for the growth and transition of such regional integration arrangements from ordinary supra-national organizations to regional states. The Draft Treaty states clearly in Article 2 (1) that the contracting Parties intend to establish among themselves an East African Community and as

---

[66] Mvungi, S.E.A infra (1994) at p. 22

an integral part of such a community a common market, subsequently a monetary Union and eventually a *political federation* (emphasis mine). It is concluded therefore that the character of the new integration arrangement is not to establish economic cooperation alone, but to achieve political union of a federal form as the final goal. In view of the political goal of the EAC, it follows that the provisions of the Draft Treaty must be construed within the context of the final goal, to wit, the achievement of the political federation. The analysis of the Draft Treaty, which shall follow hereunder, adheres to this theoretical scheme.

ESTABLISHMENT AND MEMBERSHIP OF EAC

Like the former EAC, the new East African Community is an international organization aimed at achieving Economic integration of the East African Region. According to Article 2 (1) which establishes the Community, a phase-to-phase approach at integration is envisaged, namely the establishment of the Common market, monetary Union and finally a political federation. The addition of the two last phases, namely the monetary Union and eventually a political federation, marks a sharp contrast the present draft treaty from the establishment provision of the dissolved East African Community.[67] The treaty of the former EAC envisaged the common market as the final goal of the Cooperation. This implied that contracting states did not envisage that the integration arrangement would finally supersede them by the creation of an East African State.

The agreement by the three East African States, Kenya, Uganda and Tanzania, to work towards an East African federation is without doubt the most important event in the 20th Century history of the people of East Africa. For the first time the leaders and the led are speaking the same language. The Federation of East Africa will create a powerful state and economy which will change the geo-politics of the region. The potential is enormous and the people rather than the states stand to gain from this initiative. If the federation is achieved Tanzania's nascent capitalist economy stands to gain from the integrated East African market. In fact ten years of such a community, a movement towards the Federation of East, Central and Southern African States bringing all SADC States under one regional State

---

[67] See Article 2 (1) of the treaty for East Africa Co-operation.

could be an achievable dream because the East African Federation would inevitably be a member of SADC as long as Tanzania is a member of both.

It is also important to point out that a new EAC makes sense only in the context of its federal objective, otherwise Tanzania should continue with SADC and COMESA and reject the EAC as an unnecessary duplication. One should note that even at that time when the dissolved East African Community was being established some individual leaders of the three contracting states still harboured the idea of an East African federation. In fact the dissolution of the East African Currency Board and the creation of Central Banks for each member state were all a result of the failure by the East African states to agree on the question of the federation. Mwalimu Nyerere told the Tanzanian National Assembly that:

> "There is another important change taking place in our economic affairs which will affect the whole future of our development. Tomorrow Tanzanian currency notes will be issued for the first time and in August Tanzanian coins will be issued. These will gradually replace the East African notes and coins which are at present the means of exchange in the country. They will be issued at par - that is to say that anyone taking East African notes or coins to a bank will be given an equivalent amount of Tanzanian money.
>
> This change was not decided upon for prestige reasons. The decision was made because it is impossible to plan economic development properly if currency and credit are not within the control of the planners - that is, of the government.
>
> Had an East African Federation been inaugurated, East African Currency could have continued. Indeed, if federation does come in the future, the currencies of the countries involved will have to be re-merged. But for the present our Tanzanian Currency is essential to us".[68]

The contracting states of the East Africa Community are Tanzania, Kenya and Uganda.[69] In article 2 (4) and 2 (5) the Draft Treaty makes provisions for accession to the treaty as a member or an associate or participant in the activities of the community. These are perhaps among the most unsatisfactory provisions of the Draft Treaty. It was expected that the provisions of Article 2 (5)that lay down conditions *sine qua non* for admission of a foreign country to the community as a member, associate or a participant should have laid

---

[68] Speech to the National Assembly of Tanzania, June 13, 1966: The Nationalist, Dar es Salaam June 14, 1966 pg. 7.

[69] Art. 2 (3) of the Draft Treaty

down specific conditions for each category of members. A foreign country which wants to be associated or to participate in one or more of the activities of the Community need not be subjected to similar conditions as one that seeks admission as a member. It would seem that the conditions laid down by Article 2 (5) are applicable to those states that seek full membership of the Community. They are however unsuitable for application to those states that seek only associate or participatory relationship with the community.

In any event, it has transpired in the public media, a fact that has not been denied by the East African Cooperation secretariat, that some neighbouring states, including Rwanda, have already applied for membership. It is not known which category of membership has been applied for but, be that as it may, the wisdom of admitting new members at this stage is doubtful. The three states Kenya, Uganda and Tanzania have to integrate into a community first before they can admit new members under any category of membership. There are many problems that have to be resolved amongst the three member states, before new members with new problems can be admitted. For instance, Uganda has yet to democratize its politics. Its no party system does not sit well with the generally accepted norms of democratic governance. So it is to be envisaged that the signing of the treaty will enable the two Partner States to encourage Uganda to democratize further its political system. Furthermore, Uganda is still facing internal strife in the form of rebel war. It is natural that the community activities cannot prosper if peace and tranquillity are not restored in Uganda. Therefore while such serious problems remain to be resolved within the community, new members like Rwanda, Burundi, Sudan or Somalia, all of which have serious political problems, cannot be admitted into the community. The confusion that will ensue will render the community a non-starter.

LEGAL CAPACITY

The legal capacity of the community is provided for under Article 3. Article 3 (1) states *inter alia* that the community shall have the capacity within each of the Partner Status of a body corporate with perpetual succession and shall have power to acquire, hold, manage and dispose of land and other property, and to sue and be sued in its own name.

Article 3 (2) provides further that the community shall have power to perform any of the functions conferred upon it by the treaty and to do all other things including borrowing that are necessary or desirable for its performance of those functions. Article 3(3) provides that pursuant to its cooporate status the community shall be represented by its Secretary General. These provisions are too scanty for a supra-national body that is intended to grow and coalesce into a regional state. A new Article 3 (4) should be added with a view to providing for direct application of community law and decisions in the domestic jurisdiction of the Partner States. This will mean that the process of incorporation of community law, policies and decisions be done away with, as that would impede the growth and development of the community as a supra-national body.

Furthermore, it is important for purposes of clarity to insert a provision stating that in its areas of jurisdiction, the community law, policies and decisions shall be exclusive and supreme vis-à-vis any national law, decision and/or policy of the member states. The wisdom of adding these provisions not only mitigates the negative schools of our experiences of failure in the dissolved East African Community but also impresses upon the political leadership of the member states on the special status of the East Africa Community as a supra-national body aiming at superseding the statehood of the member states.

In contrast with any ordinary provisions of international Organisations, the Draft Treaty intends to create its own legal and constitutional system at the East African level. After its signification and coming into force, the Treaty will in reality establish East African legal and constitutional order separate and superior to that of the individual member states. East African law will become directly applicable, enforceable and binding on the domestic jurisdiction of each member state. The executive, legislature and judicature of the member state shall cease to exercise sovereign power over areas of competence vested in the community organs. They will however be bound to apply, enforce and/or implement East African law as the supreme law of the East African community. In a word, a supra-national competence and structure will have begun to turn East Africa into a new domestic sphere under the community. The new legal order shall be binding upon both the states and their nationals. Nationals of each member state shall acquire directly enforceable rights and duties under the community law and their participation in community affairs shall be direct and not through their states.[70]

---

[70] Mvungi, (1994) at pg 37-43

OBJECTIVES OF THE COMMUNITY

The Draft Treaty has attempted to avoid reproduction of the objectives of the COMESA Treaty. In doing so however its Article 4 (3) (a) fails to focus on any sectoral priority that the integration arrangements seek to develop and/or improve. The COMESA Treaty states in Article 3 (a) that one of the main objectives of COMESA shall be to attain sustainable growth and development of the member states by promoting balanced and harmonious development marketing structures.

The COMESA hardly aims at political union as its immediate or long-term objective. But for a community which aims at political union the creation or establishment of production and marketing capacities of the people of East Africa should have been stated clearly as the first objective. The treaty should provide a vision of an integrated economy for East Africa as a building block of an economically strong Federation.

In this regard East Africans want to hear that, contrary to the politically bankrupt economic politicies of the three members states, the community shall become their saviour. It shall dedicate itself to deliberate economic policies aimed at building the investment capacity of individual East Africans with a view to creating a strong local entrepreneurial class capable of producing for the consumer needs of East Africans and for the export market. To talk about the creation of export economy without dealing with the consumer need of the local population is to beg the question . In any event a provision should be made to the effect that the community shall take deliberate remedial measures to stimulate economic growth in the Partner States that are at lower levels of economic development in order to bring their economies to be level with those of more developed Partner States. Levelling and/or equalization of economic development will go a long way in curing the ills that caused the collapse of the former East African Community and shall make the common market, the monetary union and finally the Federation achievable goals. This proposition contradicts the principle of variable Geometry which is both elitist and academic. A small community of three States cannot effectively apply the principle of variable Geometry as is the case in big integration arrangements like COMESA and SADC. In any case the final goal of COMESA and SADC is not political Union as the East African Community. To create differentiated development within a Federal state is a recipe for collapse.

Implementation of Treaty

In view of the discussion on the supra-national character of the East African Community and the necessity to provide for direct application of East African Law, it is unnecessary to provide for incorporation of community legislation into the domestic law of the Partner States. Therefore Article 7 (2) should be deleted.

Institutional Arrangement

The Draft Treaty establishes seven organs of the Community; namely the Summit, the Council, the Co-ordination Committee, Sectoral Committee, the East African Community Court, the East African Community Assembly and the Secretariat. This institutional arrangement shows little difference from that of SADC or COMESA and is hardly suitable for a supra-national body as envisioned in the Treaty. The basic institutions should be tailored to reflect the supra-national character of the organization and the need to respond flexibly and develop into actual state institutions of the Federation. In this regard the following changes are proposed:

Summit

This should have very few executive powers. Article 10 (6) should be changed to read:

> "An act of the Community may make provision of delegation of powers vested in any organ of the Community to any official or subordinate organ of the Community".

The Summit or the Council should have no legislative powers. All legislative powers should be vested in the East African Legislative Assembly.

Article 10 (10) should be changed to read: "The summit shall cause its decisions made pursuant to this Treaty to be given legislative effect by the Legislative Assembly."

This is to remove from the Summit the power to enact law or rules and orders that are binding in law. This is in line with rules of democratic governance. The idea is to subject decisions of the Summit to the will of the people through the Legislative Assembly.

The Council

This should be named "Council of East African Ministers" as in the dissolved East African Community Treaty.[71] The composition of the Council should change so that the Summit has power to appoint from a list submitted by the Head of State of each Partner Country an equivalent number of Ministers in accordance with the portfolios created by the Treaty. Ministers responsible for Regional cooperation in each Partner State should be *ex-officio* members of the Council but no other Minister of the Partner State should be a member of the Council of East African Ministers. The idea should be to create an East African Cabinet. In this regard each East African Minister should be assisted by a professional staff headed by a permanent secretary.

East African Community Court

This should be named the "Supreme Court of East Africa". The present Draft Treaty provisions envisage a community court that is too narrow to be able to suit the needs of a supra-national community. Left as it is the East African Community Court is like the SADC or COMESA court suitable only for an international organization of such a type.

It is envisioned that a Supreme Court of East Africa shall be both a community court as provided for in Article 18 and an appellate Court of last resort for cases emanating from the Courts of Appeal of the Partner States. It is proposed therefore that Articles 18, 22, and 25 should be changed to provide for the role of the Court as a supreme court of Appeal. The need to have such a court is obvious because the courts of Appeal of the Partner States have so far failed to fill the gap left by the former East African Court of Appeal. Presently the courts of Appeal of the Partner Status have earned for themselves the notorious reputation of "courts of technicalities" rather than final courts of justice. A need for a more bold court of last resort therefore justifies the creation of a court of higher calibre. Further, the competence of the East Africa court should be extended to include entertaining Appeals on human rights violations. It will be proposed elsewhere in this study that the Community Treaty should either incorporate a regional human rights convention, or provide for its conclusion immediately after the signing of the Draft Treaty. The High Courts of the Partner States should have original jurisdiction over breach of the East Africa Human rights convention, the Appellate courts of the Member States should be courts of 1st Appeal and the supreme Court of East Africa should exercise final Appellate powers.

The East African Community Assembly

This organ should be named the "East African Legislative Assembly," which was the name given originally the Treaty of the former East African Community and it more precisely defines the functions of this organ of the community than just referring to it as the East African Community Assembly.

Article 44 (1) (a) providing that the Assembly shall be constituted with 27 elected members should be changed to remove the definite number of members so as to have some flexibility in case the need arises to enlarge the number or a new member state is admitted to the Community.

Furthermore, Article 44 (2) and 49 should be changed so that the Chairman of the Legislative Assembly is styled "Speaker" instead of "Chairman"

Regarding the functions of the Legislative Assembly, the provisions of Article 45 should be changed so that the first function of the Assembly should be enacting laws for the East African Community in the areas of competence vested in the community.

The current Article 45 (1) should be amended to state clearly that the Assembly shall discuss and deliberate on all matters pertaining to the Community. A new Article 45 (2) should provide for direct applicability of Acts of the East African Legislative Assembly in the domestic spheres of the member states. The current Article 45 (2) should be numbered Article 45 (4). Article 46 should be amended to remove reference to 27 members.

Article 57 should be amended in accordance with the provisions of the proposed Article 45 (2). Article 59 (3) should be amended to remove the powers of the Summit to enact laws for the East African Community. The East African Legislative Assembly should possess full legislative powers. The assent by the Presidents of East Africa should be staggered so that only the chairperson of the Summit for the current year should signify the assent.

This will create a tradition that will slowly institutionalize the East African Presidency. In accordance with this view, Article 60(1) should be deleted, since the chairperson of the Summit acts for and on behalf of the whole Summit. It is unnecessary to provide a separate form for dissent outside the Summit. If this were allowed, the very inaction that destroyed decision-making under the former East African Community shall set in and destroy the Community. Article 10(8) provides a sufficient forum to record objections in the Summit. No opportunity should be given to objections by a Head of state on community matters outside the Summit.

The Secretariat

The secretariat is the motor of the Community. It has been proposed that the functions of the Community be divided into portfolios headed by East African Ministers permanently appointed by the Summit for each legislative period. It has further been proposed that each East African Minister should be assisted by a competent professional staff headed by a permanent secretary. The permanent secretary serves as long as his good behaviour and competence continues and as prescribed in the staff regulations regarding retirement age. It is this staff that forms the East African Community Civil Service at the top of which is the Secretary General and his two deputy Secretary Generals.

It is therefore proposed that this structure be reflected clearly in the provisions of Article 63.

Provisions Relating to Areas of EAC Competence

Industrial Development

Perhaps the most frustrating provisions of the Draft Treaty relate to economic integration. The Draft Treaty is a bad copy of the COMESA Treaty in this regard. For an integration arrangement whose final goal is a political federation it was expected that priority should have been given to industrial development and cooperation than the clear over-emphasis on trade liberalization. The COMESA Treaty has 39 articles on trade liberalisation. The Draft Treaty has 36, falling short of only three. The COMESA Treaty has 7 Articles on industrial development. The Draft Treaty has only 2. One could dismiss this method of analysis as perfunctory and shallow but it is not the intention of this study to say that a multitude of legal provisions necessarily implies better ones. The point is that the copying was badly done, because even the so-called substance is hardly adequate in the two Articles that the Draft Treaty set aside for industrial development. It is proposed that the chapter on industrial development should follow immediately after chapter nine. The provisions relating to industrial development should be re-worked to provide clearly for the following:

a) An East African economic reconstruction fund. This fund should be deliberately contributed to by each member state to provide for interest free capital for indigenous East Africans who have feasible industrial/commercial projects but lack capital and collateral.

b) A strategic programme and commitment by the Community to level off the economies of the Partner States so that less developed economies are brought up to the level of the more developed ones. Such economic strategy will reduce friction, squabbles and acrimony that may cause the economically weak and less developed member states to disrupt the movement towards political integration.

c) Inward focused industrial and agrarian production strategy aimed at the satisfaction of the bulk of internal consumption needs and an aggressive and competitive export-oriented production aimed at the world market.

d) Strict environmetal protection and preservation legal regime that will make East Africa a safe home for its people.

The East African Human Rights Conventions

It is proposed that Chapter 26 should be restructured to provide for and focus on the conclusion of an East African Human Rights Convention as the centre piece of the East African Constitutional and Legal order.

The Supreme Court of East African should have, *inter alia*, power to act as the supreme appellate court in Human rights matters.

5

RECOMMENDATIONS AND VIEWS ON THE DRAFT TREATY FOR THE ESTABLISHMENT OF THE EAST AFRICAN COMMUNITY

RECOMMENDATIONS AND VIEWS ON THE INTRODUCTION TO THE DRAFT TREATY FOR EAST AFRICAN COOPERATION

1. The current international trend indicates a movement towards an integrated global economy, therefore East Africans are on the right track in attempting to revive their regional cooperation.

2. Countries engaged in structural adjustment policies may gain or lose individually during the process of regionalization but the more important challenge for East African cooperation is to strengthen the role of the private sector without weakening the role of the state as the overseer and participant in making structural reforms.

3. There is general public ignorance of the Draft Treaty, therefore time, effort and resources should be put into this area so that the people of East African enter the cooperation arrangement from the standpoint of knowledge rather than ignorance.

4. The general feeling of most people in East Africa is that the integration process is proceeding at too high a speed so that the people of East Africa are being marginalized and left behind.

5. The Draft Treaty does not allocate any role for the people in the affairs of the community and the integration process. No attempt is made to make the community accountable to the people of East Africa.

6. Interviews with diverse players in the integration process indicate that zero tariffs will benefit Kenya while Tanzania will end up as the net loser. Tanzania is expected to lose over 91 billion shillings a year if zero tariffs begin in July this year as planned.

7. The Draft Treaty does not adequately address itself to the problem of imbalance in trade and production among the three East African States. This should be done before the Draft Treaty is signed.

8. Different levels of political development of the Member States shall adversely affect the integration process. It is recommended that each Member State should sort out its internal political problems and bring itself up to acceptable regional standards rather than subject the cooperation process to the unpredictable whims of individual state leaders who may have selfish interests that may create hurdles for the new community.

9. Armed conflicts and political instability within the domestic spheres of the Member States, especially in Uganda, and the involvement of Member States in regional conflicts will subject cooperation endeavors to unknown strains. Tanzania needs to carefully consider this factor especially because those involved in armed conflicts are its neighbours.

10. The three East African States have to harmonize their land policies and laws if the question of free movement of people and resources is to be properly handled by the community.

11. The Education system in the three East African states must be harmonized in order to have a common education policy.

12. Tanzania must first carefully examine how the East African Cooperation will assist her in resolving key development issues like growing mass poverty, deterioration of social conditions and unemployment before it signs the Draft Treaty.

RECOMMENDATIONS AND VIEWS ON POLITICAL ANALYSIS OF THE TREATY FOR EAST AFRICAN COMMUNITY

1. Political cooperation enjoys a prominence in the current thinking on cooperation in East Africa that was totally lacking in the old East African Community Treaty.

2. There is a certain degree of political will on the part of the leadership in East Africa to engineer meaningful political cooperation, even though the political will is based on individualized leadership wishes rather than established public opinion.

3. The current leadership in the three Partner States deserve commendation for their support for political cooperation in the region.

4. This study has also shown that there are several areas where work still needs to be done to turn the hopes of political cooperation and even federation into a reality, namely:

   i) The idea of federation needs to be closely examined, debated and interrogated. There is a need to begin to develop different scenarios that it may take so as to familiarize the leadership and population with the possible choices, their costs and benefits.

   ii) There is a need to develop a vision for political federation. This is critical in order to sustain and reinforce the political will. As already explained, political cooperation and federation is very difficult to achieve. The leadership therefore needs to engage in what we have called the "upgrading of common interest". It needs to be shown that cooperation will not only help the effective utilization of existing resources but also the expected stimulus that it will provide in other areas. The idea of building a future economic bloc in Africa, promoting the region's bargaining power in international fora and building a powerful regional political and military power base needs to be explored.

   iii) There is a need to explore processes that may bring about the envisaged closer cooperation and ultimately federation, even more so since, as already pointed out, the East African Cooperation in its present framework is already giving rise to the phenomenon of political integration. There is therefore a need to chart strategies on how to cope with the consequences of political integration in an effort to attain a political federation.

   iv) Finally the various institutional arrangements of the community need a second look. The Assembly could yield greater benefits if it were people-centred. Also the various civil society institutions need to be assisted to associate on an East African basis.

5. After making the above general observations, the following specific recommendations can be made:

   i) The Draft Treaty should not be signed hurriedly in order to please certain interests while jeopardizing its long-term potential. If it has to be signed next month, then it should be merely a document of intent with details to come later in the form of protocols.

   ii) Following from the above, a sustained open discussion should be invoked among important groups of stakeholders, such as the parliament, trade unions, cooperatives, professional associations, NGOs, religious organizations and all other relevant civil society bodies.

   iii) Efforts should be made to make the end-product of the community inward looking, people-oriented/centred and socially broad-based.

   iv) Institutionally, the most important decision-making body of the community should be the East African Assembly elected directly by the people of East Africa rather than the Summit of presidents. This is not only because the Assembly is a much more democratic body, but also because the Summit made up of three members only can be quite unstable, unpredictable, and capable of generating unnecessary friction. The creation of the new Secretariat of the Community should be reviewed with the intention of making it more democratic. Furthermore, important positions in the secretariat should be vetted by the Assembly.

RECOMMENDATION AND VIEWS ON THE ECONOMIC CONTEXT OF THE EAST AFRICAN COMMUNITY

1. Various stakeholders interviewed seem to suggest that Tanzania wants to see an "equitable development of the Partner States". Specifically Tanzania wants to carry out the following:

   a) To create conditions for rapid growth of exports;

   b) To exploit opportunities for economies of scale in infrastructure (transport and communications, energy) and services (financial institutions, education, health, water) at regional level;

   c) To support sustainable industrial development and economic diversification.

2. Conditions Leading to the Signing of the East African Treaty. During consultations a number of proposals were made. They include:

   i)   Identifying areas in the treaty which make their implementation currently difficult and proposing appropriate changes;

   ii) Including the proposed amendments in the Treaty;

   iii) Collecting people's views on the East African Cooperation Treaty;

   iv) Signing the amended Treaty.

3. Necessary Measures that would lead Tanzania to Participate Effectively and Competitively in the East African Community.

The measures are categorized into immediate, medium and long-term.

Immediate-term Measures

Form an *East African Cooperation Preparedness Unit* to be known as EACPU The secretariat of the EACPU Preparedness Unit should be located in the Ministry of Foreign Affairs and International Cooperation but should have an advisory committee which includes members from key stakeholders in government, public sector and private sector (including research institutes) from the Mainland and Zanzibar.

The major issues which the EACPU Preparedness Unit should focus on among others, include:

a) Designing ways of increasing the quantity and quality of business investment in Tanzania;

b) Encouraging operating firms to have better performance and be competitive

c) Encouraging low performing firms to maximize their potential by adopting best practices; and

d) Improving the opportunities of both large and small businesses to exploit information technology.

In order to achieve the above outputs the following activities will have to be carried out by EACPU Preparedness Unit.

a) Identify current and future constraints which impede the performance of businesses in Tanzania;

b) Prioritize the constraints for effective elimination;

c) Identify the major actors in resolving the constraints;

d) Agree on the roles of different partners (government, private sector, individuals, etc) in eliminating the constraints/bottlenecks;

e) Conduct the following studies, which would enhance the extent of Tanzania's participation and competitiveness:

- A study on the capacity building situation (Tanzania Mainland and Zanzibar) and the potential impact of free movement of labour and capital to economic development;

- A study in the opportunities of harmonizing the monetary and fiscal policies to the Tanzanian economy;

- A study on the probable gains and losses of Tanzania's participation in EACPU;

- A study on the effects of tariff reduction and how it can best be done; and

- Make the East African Treaty, a *People-Centred Economic Community* by collecting views from the private sector, civic organizations and other individual citizens.

The Medium-term Measures

i) Identify key areas in which Tanzania has a comparative advantage or are of critical importance;

ii) Identify infant industries which need protection;

iii) Establish industrial benchmarks for tariff reduction eligibility; and

iv) Invest in capacity building (software and hardware).

The Long -term Measures

i) Invest in capacity building (software and hardware);

ii) Improve infrastructure and economic services; and

iii) Improve productive sectors.

CRITICAL ISSUES ON TRADE

Insufficient Data Base

It has been established that Tanzania is not in a position to monitor her participation and developments in the East African Cooperation due to an insufficient data base.

It is therefore recommended that Tanzania should invest in capacity building and build a sufficient data base for quantifying her participation in the EAC.

Elimination of Import duties for Imports from Partner States (Zero Tariff Rate by July 31, 1999) and Agree on Common External Tariff

This study has found out the following constraints:

a) Significant government revenue loss from import duties if zero tariff rate is imposed by July 31, 1999 and its implications on Tanzania's cash budget system.

b) The formula of how the customs revenue would be shared is not known.

c) Loss of revenue arising from the use of cheaper imports if internal tariffs are eliminated while external tariffs differ among Partner States.

It is recommended that the elimination of import duties should be gradual and there should be harmonization of external tariffs. The draft treaty for EAC needs to explicitly show the mechanism of sharing the customs revenue.

CRITICAL ISSUES ON AGRICULTURE

Low Productivity Levels in Agriculture

Current productivity in Tanzanian agriculture measured by cereal yields per hectare is lower than in the Partner States. It is therefore recommended that Tanzania should cooperate with the Partner States in developing technologies and extension messages, which are relevant for the development of the agricultural sector.

Poor Rural Transport Network

The majority of rural people walk long distances to and from the markets and other service centres. It is therefore recommended that Tanzania should develop rural road network for making the agricultural sector more dynamic and productive.

CRITICAL ISSUES ON INDUSTRY

Most Tanzanian Industries Cannot Survive in the Event of Competing with Similar Products From Partner States

It has been observed that the costs of production are too high because of high utility costs, taxes and poor infrastructure. It has also been observed that Tanzania lacks dynamic entrepreneurial sector. The following recommendations are as therefore being made:

a) Gradually reduce the protective rates for locally-produced products;

b) Seriously address the problem of infrastructure (roads, railways, air transport, telecommunications);

c) Invest in capacity building of entrepreneurial sector;

d) Diversify the industrial base;

e) Financial institutions should provide support to indigenous entrepreneurs through development and export finance; and

f) Study the impact of taxes on industrial competitiveness and performance.

Development of Small and Medium-scale Industries

This study has found out that there is lack of concrete measures to facilitate small and medium scale industries in Tanzania. It is being recommended that Tanzania should do the following:

a) Clearly define a policy on small and medium-scale enterprises (SME).

b) Define strategy and specific actions to stimulate the development of the SME sector.

Harmonization and Rationalization of Investment Incentives

The quantitative investment incentives are not uniform in the three partner states. It is therefore recommended that each Partner State should improve the current incentives (tax holidays, licensing procedures, financial infrastructure, etc.).

Cooperation in Standardization and Quality Assurance

Tanzania lacks a comprehensive national policy on matters of quality, standardization and testing. It is therefore recommended that Tanzania should do the following:

i) Strengthen the legal framework on these issues;

ii) Accredit internationally the Tanzania Bureau of Standards so that her certificates are recognized worldwide.

CRITICAL ISSUES ON TRANSPORT

Economic Infrastructure

Tanzania is suffering from Poor Infrastructure in general. It is recommended that urgent measures should be taken to improve telecommunication services and also to increase the number and length of paved roads.

CRITICAL ISSUES ON TOURISM AND NATURAL RESOURCES

Common Tourism Promotion Policy/Strategy

The present state of the tourist industry in East Africa reveals the following problems:

a) Contradictory tourism strategies (high volume, mass tourism versus low volume environmentally friendly, quality tourism).

b) Different levels of infrastructure and superstructure of Partner States.

c) Undefined formula for sharing equitably the revenue from tourism.

It is therefore recommended that the three states should harmonize their policies on tourism and harmonize the development of infrastructure in the three partner states.

RECOMMENDATIONS AND VIEWS ON LEGAL PROVISIONS OF THE DRAFT TREATY

1. The East African coooperation is an age old aspiration of the people of East Africa. The colonial power that ruled East African states was not the originator of cooperation among East African peoples. It is this age-old cooperation among the people of East Africa that became the foundation upon which the colonial power established common services that led to the creation of the East African. High Commission and later the East African Common Services Organization.

2. The failure of the Post-Independence governments to establish the East African Federation was a regrettable set-back in the struggle for political and socio-economic emancipation of the people of East Africa. This failure repeated itself when the economic cooperation created in lieu of the federation in the form of an economic community collapsed.

3. The collapse of the former East African Community was a result of its failure to involve the people of East Africa in community affairs and to share equally the benefits of the community. These lessons must be taken into account in the current efforts to re-establish a new East African Community.

4. Since the proposed East African Cooperation aims finally at creating an East African State in the form of federation, East Africans must not only learn from the failure to achieve thus goal in 1963, but must deliberately tailor the new Treaty to this primary objective. This cautious approach to the question of the re-establishment of the East African cooperation has to address the following issues:

   i)   The growth and consolidation of narrow national identity even though such identity is not matched with credible economic performance.

   ii) The establishment of competing and overlapping regional integration arrangements, i.e. COMESA and SADC, of which not all East African states are members.

   iii) Political liberalization and/or democratization process that has been created.

   iv) Break-out of war and/or inter-state conflicts among or involving members of the East African cooperation.

5. In regard to 4(1) – (iv) above the following recommendations are being made:

   i)   That in order that the new community should survive and achieve the objectives it has set out in the Treaty, provisions must be made obliging the community to ensure that the majority of its programmes involve the people of East Africa. The Treaty should s establish a cooperation of the people rather than bureaucratic institutions between East African States.

   ii) That COMESA and SADC are credible regional integration arrangements that need no replication. The East African Cooperation makes no sense unless it commits itself substantially to the objective of a political federation in the shortest time possible.

iii) That each member state must set out minimum standards of political liberalization/democratization to which each member state must be committed itself to achieve within five years from the date of signing of the treaty. These standards must include good governance, plural/ liberal democracy, human rights and elimination of violence and corruption.

iv) Those member states of the East African Community should commit themselves to a common defence and security program and refrain from launching inter-state conflicts. They should also refrain from involvement in wars or conflicts with other neighbouring states.

6. The provisions of the Draft Treaty on accession to the East African Community Treaty are ambivalent and unreal. Articles 2(4) and 2(5) should be redrafted to distinguish between different categories of membership, namely a full member, an observer, an associate member and a participant.

7. The Draft Treaty should further lay down conditions for admission to any of these categories of membership.

8. It is further recommended that although some neighbouring countries may have or may wish to apply for membership of the EAC, it is too early to admit any country to the community, which should first be established between the three East African states and problems that impede cooperation between the three states resolved before new members with diverse new problems are allowed to join the community.

9. Article 3 of the Draft Treaty should be redrafted to add a new sub-article 3(4) providing for the supra-national states of the community and to provide further that legislative Acts of the Community's legislative Assembly shall have direct application in the domestic jurisdictions of the member states without requirement of incorporation.

10. Article 3 should be redrafted further to add a new sub-article 3(5) providing clearly that the community shall have exclusive jurisdiction and supremacy vis-à- vis the member states in all areas of competence reserved to it.

11. Provisions on economic objectives of the EAC Treaty should be redrafted to emphasize the need to build up the production capacity of the economies with the present over-emphasis on trade.

12. Deliberate remedial measures aimed at equalization of economic development of the Partner States have to be envisaged and provided for in the Treaty.

13. In view of proposals for a new Article 3(4), Article 7(2) of the Draft Treaty should be deleted.

14. The institutional arrangement of the EAC should reflect the supra-national character of the EAC namely:

Summit
- The Summit should remain the highest organ in the Community but should not all powers, namely executive, legislative and judicial powers should be concentrated in it.

- Sub-article 10(6) should be redrafted so that Acts of the community can delegate powers vested in any organ of the Community.

- Sub-article 10((10) should be redrafted to oblige the Summit to cause all its decisions made pursuant to the Treaty to be given legislative effect by the legislative assembly.

The Council
- The council should be re-named "council of East African Ministers" an evolving concept of an East African Cabinet of Ministers.

- The composition of the council should be an equivalent number of Ministers from each Partner State, each manning a portfolio designated in accordance with areas of competence of the Community.

- Each Head of State should submit a list of nominees who shall then be appointed by the Summit.

- East African Ministers shall not be members of the government or cabinets of the Partner States.

- Partner States Ministers responsible for regional cooperation or any other Ministers of the Partner States deemed necessary for deliberations of the council shall attend the Council of Ministers Meetings by invitation as *ex-officeio* members.

The East African Community Court

- It is recommended that a new sub-article 18(1) should be added to designate this court as the "Supreme Court of East Africa."

- A new sub-article 18(2) should be added to vest in this court original jurisdiction in matters relating to the interpretation of the Treaty of the East African cooperation and appellate jurisdiction in matters arising from East African legislative Acts and matters relating to the East African Human Rights Convention.

- Further, a new sub-article 18(3) should be added to provide for a judicial system for East African by vesting in the High Courts of the Member states original competence to hear matters arising from the application of East African Legislative Acts and the East African Human Rights Convention.

- Finally a new sub-article 18(4) should be added to the Draft Treaty to vest in the Courts of the Member States competence as Courts of First Appeal in matters arising from East African Human Rights Convention and East African Legislative Acts.

The East African Community Assembly

This organ should be named the "East African Legislative Assembly" which was the name given originally by the Treaty of the former East African Community and it more precisely defines the functions of this organ of the community than just referring to it as the East African Community Assembly.

Article 44 (1) (a) providing that the Assembly shall be constituted with 27 elected members should be changed to remove the definite number of members so as to have some flexibility in case the need arises to enlarge the number or a new member state is admitted to the Community.

Furthermore, Article 44 (2) and 49 should be changed so that the Chairman of the Legislative Assembly is styled "Speaker" instead of "Chairman."

Regarding the functions of the Legislative Assembly, the provisions of Article 45 should be changed so that the first function of the Assembly should be enacting laws for the East Africa Community in the areas of competence vested in the community.

The current Article 45 (1) should be amended to state clearly that the Assembly shall discuss and deliberate on all matters pertaining to the Community. A new Article 45 (2) should provide for direct applicability of

Acts of the East African Legislative Assembly in the domestic spheres of the member states. The current Article 45 (2) should be numbered as Article 45 (4). Article 46 should be amended to remove reference to 27 members.

Article 57 should be amended in a Cordance with the provisions of the proposed Article 45 (2). Article 59 (3) should be amended to remove the powers of the Summit to enact laws for the East African Community. The East African Legislative Assembly should possess full legislative powers. The assent by the Presidents of East Africa should be staggered so that only the chairperson of the Summit for the current year should signify the assent.

This will create a tradition that will slowly institutionalize the East African Presidency. In accordance with this view, Article 60(1) should be deleted, since the chairperson of the Summit acts for and on behalf of the whole Summit. It is unnecessary to provide a separate form for dissent outside the Summit. If this were allowed, the very inaction that destroyed decision-making under the former East African Community shall set in and destroy the Community. Article 10(8) provides a sufficient forum to record objections in the Summit. No opportunity should be given to objections by a Head of state on community matters outside the Summit.

The Secretariat

The secretariat is the motor of the Community. It has been proposed that the functions of the community be divided into portfolios headed by East African Ministers permanently appointed by the Summit for each legislative period. It has further been proposed that each East African Minister should be assisted by a competent professional staff headed by a permanent secretary. The permanent secretary serves as long as his good behaviour and competence continues and as prescribed in the staff regulations regarding retirement age. It is this staff that forms the East African Community Civil Service at the top of which is the Secretary General and his two deputy Secretary Generals.

It is therefore proposed that this structure be reflected clearly in the provisions of Article 63.

Provisions Relating to Areas of EAC Competence

Industrial Development

Perhaps the most frustrating provisions of the Draft Treaty relate to economic integration. The Draft Treaty is a bad copy of the COMESA Treaty in this regard. For an integration arrangement whose final goal is a political federation it was expected that priority should have been given to industrial development and cooperation than the clear over-emphasis on trade liberalization. The COMESA Treaty has 39 articles on trade liberalization. The Draft Treaty has 36, falling short of only three. The COMESA Treaty has 7 Articles on industrial development. The Draft Treaty has only 2. One could dismiss this method of analysis as perfunctory and shallow but it is not the intention of this study to say that a multitude of legal provisions necessarily implies better ones. The point is that the copying was badly done, because even the so-called substance is hardly adequate in the two Articles that the Draft Treaty set aside for industrial development. It is proposed that the chapter on industrial development should follow immediately after chapter nine. The provisions relating to industrial development should be re-worked to provide clearly for the following:

a) An East African economic reconstruction fund. This fund should be deliberately contributed to by each member state to provide for interest-free capital for indigenous East Africans who have feasible industrial/commercial projects but lack capital and collateral.

b) A strategic programme and commitment by the Community to level off the economies of the Partner States so that less developed economies are brought up to the level of the more developed ones. Such economic strategy will reduce friction, squabbles and acrimony that may cause the economically weak and less developed member states to disrupt the movement towards political integration.

c) Inward focused industrial and agrarian production strategy aimed at the satisfaction of the bulk of internal consumption needs and an aggressive and competitive export-oriented production aimed at the world market.

d) Strict environmental protection and preservation legal regime that will make East Africa a safe home for its people.

The East African Human Rights Conventions
It is proposed that Chapter 26 should be restructured to provide for and focus on the conclusion of an East African Human Rights Convention as the centre piece of the East African Constitutional and Legal order.

The Supreme Court of East African should have, *inter alia*, power to act as the supreme appellate court in Human rights matters.

15. The Chapter 23 providing for investment and Industrial development, Chapter 18 providing for Agriculture and Food Security, Chapter 19 providing for cooperation in environment and natural resources and Chapter 20 providing for cooperation in tourism and wildlife management should all be combined to form a master chapter on Agro-Industry development, tourism, wildlife and natural reserves management.

- A sub-article should be added in (1) above to provide for an East African economic reconstruction fund to provide for capital for empowering indigenous entrepreneurs.

- A provision should be made to ensure that economies of the member States are brought up to the same level in terms of development.

- A provision should also be made to ensure observance of a strict environmental protection legal regime so that East Africa remains a safe home for its people.

16. It is recommended that chapter 26 of the Draft Treat should be redrafted to provide for the conclusion of a separate East African Convention on Human Rights as a central pillar of the East African Constitutional and legal order.

17. The proposed Supreme Court of East Africa should have, *inter alia*, power to entertain final appeal on human rights issues.